What others have to say

"This is the most comprehensive guide for parents and other adults responsible for the care of children that I have ever seen. Beginning with the crucially important question 'What do your really want for your children?' the book moves from creating a sense of security to strengthening a sense of identity, to inspiring a life purpose—to meeting the needs of unique children. This is a very important contribution."

Psychologist Nathaniel Branden, Ph.D.

"This book provides an exciting new way to approach parenting, based on years of practical experience and research. It really demonstrates how parents can develop those human qualities most of us would like to see in our children. The ideas and suggestions provided are practical, helpful, and sound. The chapter on helping children with unique problems and needs is especially valuable."

Jack Canfield, M.Ed., Self-Esteem Seminars,
Coauthor of *Chicken Soup for the Soul*(R) series

"Reasoner and Lane have undertaken the challenge of drawing upon research and professional experience to write a book, not about discipline or achievement, but rather the more rewarding task of increasing the chances that your child will become a responsible young adult with the traits and characteristics you value most. I strongly recommend this book not only for parents, but also for teachers, school administrators, and all those interested in the growth and maturity of young people."

Dr. Jack McKay, Professor Emeritus
University of Nebraska at Omaha

"The most profound responsibility we human beings ever undertake is to parent a child. Yet how little precious preparation we are given to ready us for this challenge. Bob Reasoner and Marilyn Lane's *Parenting with Purpose* is the most deeply insightful parenting handbook I have seen. It smartly grounds the process in a parent's own sense of self, identity, and self-esteem, and in that parent's awareness regarding the values and virtues they hope their child will grow up to embody. In fact, it amounts to a blueprint for the most healthy and valuable parenting—parenting from the inside out!"

Senator John Vasconcellos
California State Senate

"*Parenting with Purpose* offers warm and readable suggestions to help you reach your parenting goals in a mindful and deliberate way. Here are simple and practical ways to build your children's internal controls and self-discipline, while encouraging the development of all those wonderful qualities you want in your children."

Author Jane Bluestein, Ph.D., author of *Parents, Teens & Boundaries,*
The Parent's Little Book of Lists: Do's and Don'ts of Effective Parents,
and *Creating Emotionally Safe Schools*

"Bob Reasoner and Marilyn Lane's years of research and experience make them uniquely qualified to write this book for parents. Their ideas are based on solid theory and offer sound, effective ways for developing what matters most: raising our children to become capable and competent human beings. I'm certain that this outstanding guide will become a valuable resource for parents. It's certainly a most-needed one."

Author Michele Borba, E.D, author of *Don't Give Me that Attitude, Building Moral Intelligence*, and others

"Not just another book on parenting... the wisdom and practical how-to's *Parenting with Purpose* provides will help you become the parent you're capable of becoming. The insights of these two authors have been field tested and proven. By applying these principles you will give your children a gift that will last a lifetime.

Bob "Hope" Moawad, Founder and CEO of Edge Learning Institute

"After over 40 years of working with children, teachers and parents I believe that no one is doing a good job of helping parents teach their children—not schools, not churches, not adult education programs, not colleges, not anyone. This book is a complete and comprehensive guide for parents. It is conceptually well-founded. It has been personalized with the authors' own experiences and it includes many suggested activities for parents to use with their children. I wish such a book had been available when we raised our children and that I could have recommended to parents in the many schools and districts where I served."

William D. Grafft, Ph.D., Retired Superintendent, Mountain View School District, California

"*Parenting with Purpose* conveys so much practical wisdom in a very easy-to-understand manner. It is action-oriented, with specific suggested activities to help the reader-parent apply the authors' principles. Frequent review of this book and putting the methods in practice should help parents, grandparents, and others caring for children be effective and raise their children with the qualities most valued."

Polly Peters, Parent and Grandparent

"I believe this book will be a significant contribution to all who read it. I especially enjoyed the personal vignettes. The concepts and suggestions are sound and will be of great value to parents."

Rita Hemsley, Ph.D., Director, ORCA Christian School

"*Parenting with Purpose* is the definitive 'instruction book' for families. Like a well-written travel guide, this book pinpoints the roadblocks and provides the maps to help your family choose the destination and truly enjoy the parenting journey. If there is room in your library for only one parenting guide, this should be it!"

Kate Gamble, Parent

Parenting with Purpose

Five Keys
to Raising Children
with Values and Vision

A Complete Guide for Parents,
Grandparents, and Caregivers

Robert W. Reasoner and Marilyn L. Lane

PERSONHOOD PRESS

Parenting with Purpose:
Five Keys to Raising Children with Values and Vision

Published by:
Personhood Press
PO Box 370
Fawnskin, CA 92333
800-429-1192
info@personhoodpress.com
www.personhoodpress.com

PERSONHOOD PRESS

ISBN 10: 1-932181-25-3
ISBN 13: 9781932181258

Library of Congress Control Number: 2007926292

Book Cover Design by: Linda Jean Thille, Blackstone Arts
Text Design by: Linda Jean Thille, Blackstone Arts

Printed in the United States of America

Dedication

We would like to dedicate this book to our children and grandchildren from whom we learned so much: Bob's family of Kathryn, Sharon, David, Wendy, Bruce, Ann, and grandsons Frank, Ryan, and Robbie, and to Marilyn's family—Lewis, David, Sue, Laura, and grandchildren Sarah, Garrett, Sharla, and LP.

ॐ ॐ ॐ

꒰ ꒰ ꒰

Acknowledgments

We would like to acknowledge the many individuals who have provided us with inspiration, friendship, and support—especially Michele Borba, Jane Bluestein, Nathaniel Branden, John Vasconcellos, Betty Hatch, Murray White, and Veronica deAndres. We deeply appreciate Greta Bratov for providing us with the opportunities to implement our program in Slovenia and Eastern Europe, Fawzi Jammal for his support in the Middle East, and Ranjit Malhi for his support in Malaysia. We are especially indebted to Jack Canfield for his guidance, friendship, and financial support of our efforts over the years.

We owe much to the support, wisdom, and patience of our partners Nancy and Clark that enabled us to conduct our work and take the time to write this. Their encouragement and understanding has made this all possible.

We would like to thank Paula Baldwin for her encouragement, her sharing of information and her experience with foster children. We need to express our thanks to David Simpson and Denise Keller for their information and assistance in writing the chapter on special needs. We also thank Barbara Clark and Judy Roseberry and other members of the California Association for the Gifted for inspiration and wisdom about parenting gifted children. We also appreciate Leon Canerot for his early work on parenting and parent education (*Tips on Parenting Strategies*), along with the many parents throughout the world who listened to our parenting ideas and encouraged us to write them down.

We appreciate the advice and counsel of Bill Grafft and Jack McKay, and we would like to give special thanks to Brad and Cathy Winch for serving as our publishers and guiding us through the process of preparing our book for publication. We greatly appreciate Linda Thille who not only designed the cover but did all the layout of our material.

Finally, we owe a debt of deep gratitude to our parents and extended families who provided us with the warmth, love, and sense of family that enabled each of us to draw from personal experience.

Table of Contents

Chapter 9 Meeting the Needs of Gifted Children 159

Chapter 10 Foster Parenting 171

Chapter 11 Becoming the Parent You Want to Be ...185

Biographical Information on the Authors 204

Foreword

We have written this book in response to the many requests from parents and educators whom we have met at workshops and conferences throughout the world. The ideas included began with the concepts developed by Bob Reasoner, a school administrator in the San Francisco Bay Area, and Dr. Stanley Coopersmith, Chairman of the Department of Psychology at the University of California at Davis.

When these concepts were used with students at the school where Bob was principal, significant changes took place. The percentage of students identified as gifted on the basis on an intelligence test increased from 7% to 35%. There were fewer and fewer discipline problems each year, as students became more personally responsible. At the high school where these students joined students from six other schools, it was found that 75% of all the leaders in the high school came from that elementary school. Teachers reported that they could always identify students from that particular school because they were more highly motivated and had long-term goals for their lives.

జ్రా జ్రా జ్రా

In 1979, Bob was appointed as superintendent of an urban school district with eight schools and a student population of 3500 students, 43% of whom were considered to be from minority cultures. Sixty-six percent of the students were not living with their two original parents, as the district had a high percentage of single-parent families. Bob began training principals and teachers in these concepts, and developed policies and processes that fostered high self-esteem among students and staff. As a result, achievement scores increased to the point where the district was designated as the highest-achieving school district out of 29 districts. All eight schools were designated as "Distinguished Schools" by the California State Department of Education. Student attendance increased to an average of 99.7% per day. Teacher absenteeism was reduced to 4.1 days per year, including sick leave. The dropout rate at the high school level declined to 5.4%, less that half that of surrounding high schools, while the percentage of students continuing their education at the college or university level increased from 65% to 89%. Discipline problems significantly declined and vandalism decreased from a cost of over $16,000 per year to less than $2,000 per year. Not one K-8 student was reported to be using drugs, and no student became pregnant. Staff morale was acknowledged by other district administrators to be the highest in the County.

ಅಃ ಅಃ ಅಃ

Marilyn Lane, a teacher in the district where Bob had previously served as an assistant superintendent, helped to develop activities to implement the concepts in her classroom. She found that the ideas were also helpful to her as a parent raising four children. The concepts were ultimately incorporated and published in the program *Building Self-Esteem* in 1982 by Consulting Psychologists Press, a firm set up to publish materials for the Stanford Psychology Department. When Marilyn became a principal in the late 1980s and early '90s, she used the same principles at her schools with similar results. Since then, schools throughout the country have used the program and report a remarkable change in their students, with fewer discipline problems and a significant increase in student motivation.

A Parent Guide to accompany the program *Building Self-Esteem* was developed, and Marilyn began teaching parenting classes. Studies showed that the school program became significantly more effective when parents understood the school program and its intent and were also taught what they could do with their children at home. We found that it normally took three to four years to change the entire climate of a school to one with fewer discipline problems and greater student motivation. However, when parents became involved and applied the learned processes at home with their children, we found significant change could be accomplished in just two to three years! Parents are indeed children's first teachers and normally have twice the impact of the school. It is our belief that parenting classes should be taught along with Lamaze and diapering and feeding the baby! Surely we should put in as much time planning our parenting as we do planning our leisure time or futures.

We have implemented the program in over 20 countries throughout the world and continue to conduct training for parents and educators. Most recently, for example, the program has been implemented in over 200 schools in Europe, with rave reviews from teachers and parents. In this book, we have shared some effective strategies and activities that can be used at home. Unlike many books on parenting, it is not a book on discipline. It is a plan to build a functioning family that fosters self-esteem and develops the qualities in children _you want_ them to have. We hope the book will provide information and insights to enable you to become the person you want to be and a parent with a purpose: to raise a child with the skills, attributes, and attitudes necessary to living responsibly and successfully in the future.

We recognize that many parents have only one child, and therefore have made our suggestions in singular form. We have tried to avoid displaying any bias so therefore have used 'he' or 'she' interchangeably. We ask that you adjust the pronouns to make it appropriate for your situation.

Robert Reasoner
Marilyn Lane

৯৫ ৯৫ ৯৫

Chapter 1
Introduction

"We stand at the dawn of a new era. Before us is the most important decade in the history of civilization, a period of stunning technological innovation, unprecedented economic opportunity, and great cultural rebirth. The issue is how do we prepare our children for it."

John Naisbitt

ॐ ॐ ॐ

Being a parent can be one of the great joys of life. It also can be an awesome and frustrating responsibility. There are few roles as demanding as that of a parent. Not only are parents or grandparents entrusted with the physical well-being of their children, they also shape their children's personalities, the skills they develop, their values, their behaviors, and how they feel about themselves. Never has this been of greater significance than as we enter the 21st century because we are now experiencing a world that is changing faster than we can change the institutions entrusted with preparing our young people for that world.

As a result of the changes taking place, children will need new skills, productive attitudes, and a value system they can use to make wise decisions. They will have multiple options and choices, and will need to function effectively in surroundings quite different from anything they have known. Parents and others responsible for children must give serious thought to the qualities children should develop to enable them to cope with this changing world. According to *Fortune* magazine, business leaders indicate that these qualities should include interest in life-long learning, interpersonal skills, self-esteem, problem-solving skills, creative thinking, leadership skills, resiliency, ability to adapt to change, and initiative in addition to competency in the basic skills.

Schools cannot possibly impart all the knowledge needed for tomorrow's world. The total body of knowledge now doubles every two to three years. As many occupations become obsolete, new occupations take their place. The role of the educator has changed to one of facilitator for accessing information, collaborative learning, global interaction, and life-long learning. How does this affect your role, the role of the parent?

John Lennon once said,"Life is what happens to you in the midst of planning it." Sometimes it seems that way, but there are some important aspects of our lives that produce better results with careful planning.

Have you ever spent time with a travel professional or on the Internet planning a trip or your vacation? What about your financial planning? Planning your career and making plans for retirement means long-term planning and hours spent with professionals. Yet, parenting is something that we often let happen without much help after the Lamaze classes end. The question has often been asked, where is the manual that comes with the baby? We read books, often with conflicting advice and most often seek solutions for discipline problems after they occur. Surely, we must consider the challenge of our changing world and how it impacts our role as a parent. Parenting should require long-term planning about what the "product" should be like in adulthood in the world of tomorrow and how we can do our best to see that the children we are raising have the qualities they will need and be the people we want them to become. Whether you are a brand new parent or a seasoned veteran, this is what "parenting with purpose" is all about.

This book, *Parenting with Purpose*, is intended to help you become more conscious of those skills, habits, attitudes, behaviors, visions, and values you wish to develop in your children and to share with you some effective strategies for developing those characteristics. We hope to make you aware of the good practices you already have in place, and we will share what we have found to be effective through our experience and research as parents and educators. Because the greatest single factor affecting the development of children is the model you represent, we will also be sharing some ideas for your personal growth to help you become more effective as a parent. To begin defining your purpose, we ask you to consider the following questions:

1. What do you want for your children?
2. What were the significant events/experiences in your life that shaped you?
3. What are the qualities you believe are important and want to develop in your children?

What do you really want for your children?

What we want for our children is the major factor that determines what we encourage or discourage in our children. The characteristics we want for our children determines how we discipline, what we talk with our children about, and how they feel about themselves.

Most of us as parents want similar things for our children. When parents from many cultures were asked about the characteristics they want for their children, these are the responses received:

- Responsibility and reliability
- Ability to make good choices
- Ability to delay gratification
- Relative freedom from stress and anxiety
- Happiness
- High test scores
- Compassion
- Problem-solving ability
- Financial self-sufficiency
- Good health
- Comfort in taking risks
- Motivated in school
- Self-confident/high self-esteem
- Competence
- Concern for social justice
- Interest in being a life-long learner
- Ability to build a good marriage/love relationship

Dr. Tim Johnson, a physician and medical specialist for ABC television network, stated on TV, "A positive self-concept is more important than learning facts and figures. That's what I want for my children, at least. How they feel about their own capabilities is the foundation for what they can accomplish throughout their lives."

As authors we think it is important for children to have a sense of hope and enthusiasm for living. We hope they will have passion and excitement for what they are doing with their lives, and we hope they will have a vision for their future. We want them to have positive feelings about themselves and to act in self-assured, self-accepting ways. We believe they should have a foundation of values that support their behaviors and decision making so they have self-respect, as well as respect for others. We also hope they will be responsible and accountable for their actions.

What do you want for your children? It's important to take time to clarify what qualities you most want to develop in your children. The primary purpose of this book is to help you make this determination and then to provide some suggestions on how to foster those qualities. We have found that by being clear about these qualities you can then "parent with purpose" and increase the likelihood that your children will turn out in ways that are consistent with your dreams for them.

∞ ✿ ∞

Personal memories of significance

The best place to begin our parenting with purpose is with ourselves. We come to our role as parents bringing with us memories of our own past. We are indeed the sum of our experiences. Some of these are pleasant memories, others are painful to think about, and others are significant for various reasons. These significant memories play a large role in determining who we are, and have a major impact on our children. Therefore, it's important that we become conscious of how these experiences have shaped us as we deal with our children.

Significant events that occur in your life affect who you are ar
what's important to you. As authors we examined some of ou.
own significant events. Bob recalls that one of the traditions in
his family when he grew up was having the children of the family perform for the adults at special holidays like Easter, Thanksgiving, and Christmas. Bob recalls being embarrassed and resentful at having to prepare for this and having to play his clarinet
before his cousins, aunts, uncles, and grandparents. He remembers on one occasion even hiding in the attic to avoid having to
perform. Consequently, he never asked his own children to perform before anyone, which may or may not have been in their
best interests.

On the other hand, Marilyn remembers enjoying tap dancing
and showing off. She still loves to dance but has less need to be a
star. She also enjoyed singing in the church choir. The fact that
Bob found performing in front of others objectionable while
Marilyn thoroughly enjoyed the experience illustrates how different children are from one another.

ॐ ॐ ॐ

Often, a significant event is one of a difficult nature that creates a major change. It could be an illness, a divorce, a marriage,
a move, a change in occupations, an achievement or a disappointment.

Take some time to consider the significant events in your life
by writing them down in the following format. Review your
childhood memories and the impact they have had on who you
are today, how they affect what you do for your children, and
how it affects your parenting.

Sometimes a parent's perception of significant events may differ from that of a child. As a parent, don't be surprised if what
you consider to be a significant event in the life of your child
turns out to be insignificant to your child. Marilyn Lane's oldest
daughter, a single mom, called her not too long ago in one of her
self-searching modes. She was trying to determine the early ex-

...iences that were benchmarks in determining who she is. As ...ey spoke, experiences and benchmarks were, indeed, a matter of perception. Marilyn's perceptions of incidents and their importance were very different from her daughter's. Incidents that Marilyn, as a mother, considered important her daughter considered trivial or couldn't even remember. Likewise, her daughter's important memories typically seemed trivial to Marilyn. For example, one of her daughter's happiest recollections was having the children who lived next door over for lunch for tomato soup and grilled cheese sandwiches on a particularly cold school day. Her daughter wanted to create similar happy memories for her own children. Memories Marilyn considered most significant were those that required her effort and conscious planning. Those ranged from being her daughter's Sunday school teacher and Girl Scout leader to creating her Halloween costumes, helping with homework and attending her piano recitals. As the two of them continued to talk, it became clear to both that these experiences were all acts of love and together created a recollection of a happy childhood.

ॐ ॐ ॐ

Significant Events	Event/Experience Affect on Parenting

ॐ ॐ ॐ

What are your beliefs and values

We learn at the beginning of infancy what is valued by others and from this interaction we develop our own value system, which defines us as human beings. These beliefs and values influence our feelings, behavior, and form the basis of our personal development. These beliefs also establish our priorities and create a foundation for our decision-making. They determine where we draw a line in the sand, what we hold most dear, and what we are not willing to compromise. This is our integrity, our sense of right and wrong, our guidance system for the way we conduct ourselves as individuals, and certainly the way we parent and the values we convey to our children.

ॐ ॐ ॐ

Values differ from culture to culture, but there are similar values common to most cultures such as honesty, family loyalty, and respect for others. A journalist wrote an article for a local paper about epitaphs. In the article, he described his experience of attending a graveside service and while there he looked at the epitaphs on tombstones. As he read these, he thought about what might later be on his own tombstone. As he considered this, he wrote down the words that might best describe him, and he thought about his own legacy. He didn't like what he had written and this caused him to change the way he lived his life and his priorities. He developed goals for himself and personal rules to live by. He reported that reviewing his values and what was really most important had resulted in significant changes in his life. You might like to consider your own epitaph! What legacy will you leave? Write down some positive adjectives that describe you like caring, compassionate, competent, and creative. A friend of ours chose "a white plume" from *Cyrano de Bergerac* because, for him, it symbolized untarnished integrity and that was how he tried to live his life.

Some activities to consider:

1. Talk with your children about the values that are most important to you in making decisions for them.

2. Ask your children what values they believe are important for them to follow in planning their future.

3. Ask your older children what values they would most like to develop in their children.

A framework for developing virtues and values

You undoubtedly have strong feelings about the virtues you have acquired or developed from your childhood as well as from your experience that you consider significant. You have also developed some habits either that you feel good about or that you would like to change. Whether you like those virtues and habits or not, they will undoubtedly affect how you relate to your children and the messages that they receive from you. Being conscious of those virtues and habits enables you to work on changing them or adhering to them as you consider the goals of your parenting.

అడ అడఅ అడ

In the following chapters we will provide suggestions on how to foster specific qualities in children using the five keys, the concepts, and the process developed several years ago. This process is based upon a framework of five basic human needs: the sense of security, the sense of identity, the sense of belonging, the sense of purpose, and the sense of personal competence. We have now had several years of experience using this framework in a wide variety of situations, including schools, psychiatric institutions, hospitals, and drug and alcohol rehabilitation centers. In our research on this process we have been able to document a noticeable reduction in alcohol or substance abuse, anti-social behavior, teasing and picking on others, teenage pregnancy, eating disorders, and school truancy. In addition to reducing these deviant behaviors, parents, educators, and mental health specialists have attested to the fact that this framework has also fostered those characteristics that lead to more productive lives—qualities like responsibility, reliability, initiative, self-esteem, confidence, tolerance, and motivation.

෧ඦ෧ (වු ෧ඦ෧

We mention self-esteem because we believe it is of great importance. Abraham Maslow, the well-known psychologist, identified self-esteem as a basic human need. Since the term self-esteem has been defined in different ways we need to explain that the kind of self-esteem we are anxious to develop is healthy and authentic. It is not achieved by giving children undue praise or by developing feelings of superiority. Research has demonstrated that healthy self-esteem develops when children feel secure, have a positive sense of self, feel valued by others, and feel a sense of competence. Thus, it is not just having positive feelings about oneself. It also involves feeling competent. In order for your child, or children, to achieve healthy self-esteem they need the kind of environment and experiences that enable them to develop these feelings.

෧ඦ෧ (වු ෧ඦ෧

Since it has been our experience that individuals are much happier and feel better about themselves when their basic needs are met, we will concentrate on strategies to enable children to fulfill their critical needs for security, identity, belonging, purpose, and personal competence. By establishing the conditions to satisfy these basic needs, children are most likely to acquire those virtues and values you would like to see developed. We're convinced that this framework can be of value to you and your children.

♫ ♫ ♫

Sense of Security

This is the first of five keys to raising children with values and vision. To develop feelings of security, children must be treated with love and respect, have clear rules and expectations that are consistently enforced, and believe they have the personal power to have some control over their own lives. They also need to learn to take responsibility for their actions and accept the consequences that might result. These are the characteristics of children who lack security and those who feel secure:

Characteristics	
Children who lack feelings of security	**Children who feel secure**
Testing of limits	Responsible
Nervous	Respectful of authority
Lack of motivation	Self-disciplined
Excessively shy and fearful	Trusting of adults
Distrusting	Willing to risk failure
Defiant and disrespectful	Reliable
Stressful	Free from anxiety
Reluctant to take risks	Absence of nervous
Indecisive	symptoms
Fearful	

♫ ♫ ♫

Sense of Identity

The second key is for children to have a positive "sense of identity." This sense of identity is important because children behave in ways that are consistent with how they see themselves. Those who have positive feelings about themselves tend to relate to others in positive ways. On the other hand, those who feel inadequate or who have negative self-images are apt to relate to others in more negative ways. These are the characteristics of those who lack a positive sense of identity and those who possess a positive sense of identity:

Characteristics	
Children with negative identity	**Children with positive identity**
Over-anxious to please	Compassion and caring for others
Engage in anti-social behavior	Empathy
Expend little effort to succeed	Self-acceptance
Hypersensitive	Self-control
Temper tantrums	Consideration for others
Critical of others	Respect and tolerance for others
Seek to be the center of attention	Ability to express emotions
Lie, cheat or steal	Emotional stability
Seldom take pride in work they do	Ability to love others/ Personal worth and pride

Sense of Belonging

The third key we term a "sense of belonging." We all have the need to belong, to feel accepted and supported by others. We need to feel that we are part of a group of peers or an organization that is larger than we are. This need is first met by being part of a family that cares. To achieve this need, children must learn the social skills necessary to work cooperatively and in harmony with others, how to be a friend and how to support others. These are the characteristics of those who lack feelings of belonging and those who have a strong sense of belonging:

<u>Characteristics</u>

Children who lack strong feelings of belonging	**Children with strong feelings of belonging**
Few friends	Get along well with others
Rejected or isolated from peers	Good listening skills
Lack patience with others	Resist peer pressure
Need to be first all the time	Enjoy sharing with others
Hate to share with others	Good team member
Cruel to animals	Demonstrate leadership skills
Easily misled by peers	Feel valued by others
Bully or tease others	Good social skills
Brag or boast	Many friends
Find it hard to say "No" to peers	Contribute to welfare of others
Show off or try to impress others	

Sense of Purpose

The fourth key is to feel that the work we do and the life we lead has meaning and significance. We have called this a "sense of purpose." It comes about when children see the relevance of what they are doing and when their efforts are directed to what is significant for them. It helps when they develop a vision of what they want to achieve or what kind of person they wish to become. It also involves developing a set of values or standards to live by. These are the characteristics of those who lack a sense of purpose and those with a strong sense of purpose:

ॐ ૐ ॐ

Characteristics

Those who lack a sense of purpose	Those with a strong sense of purpose
Lack of motivation	Intellectual curiosity
Waste time	Integrity
Engage in truancy	Self-motivated
Poor grades in school	Inner satisfaction
Experiment with drugs or alcohol	Vision for their future
Disorganized	Clarity of purpose
Bored with school	Spirituality
Lack ambition	Passion for what they are doing
Few real interests	Ethical behavior
Seek thrills	Ability to risk

ॐ ૐ ॐ

Sense of Personal Competence

The fifth key is the feeling that one is competent to cope with the challenges of life, termed the "sense of personal competence." It requires a sense of independence and multiple experiences over time as well as the skills, knowledge, and attitudes necessary to be successful. These are the characteristics of those who lack feelings of competence and those with personal competence:

<u>Characteristics</u>

Those who lack feelings of competence	Those with personal competence
Make poor decisions	Personal accountability
Blame others for their failures	Decision making skills
Feel overwhelmed	Resilience
Believe they're either lucky or unlucky	Perseverance or persistence
Depend upon others for direction	Independence
	Positive outlook on life
Use poor judgment	Self-assessment skills
Easily discouraged	Knowledgeable about resources
Often fail to complete projects	Self-confidence
	Feel empowered

ॐ ॐ ॐ

This is why it is so vitally important that you as a parent be clear about the qualities you wish to develop in your children and that you purposely work to establish those conditions that foster those desired qualities. You may want to focus more on one of the keys than another because of a greater need that you perceive, or a value you believe to be more important for your child. For example, for one child, developing friendships might be a need so you would want to emphasize a sense of belonging and the development of social skills. You may believe it is important for your child to know it is okay to make mistakes and learn from them, and that they can come home, "lick their wounds," and go forth again. In this case security would be an emphasis for you.

ॐ ॐ ॐ

ໜ໌ ໜ໌ ໜ໌

Diagnostic Checklist

A Diagnostic Checklist has been provided to enable you to identify those negative qualities you currently observe in your child. Use this checklist and place a check in front of each of those qualities you see in your child now. If there are three or more checks under "Security," begin by focusing on the chapter devoted to that element. If there are fewer than three checks under "Security," move onto the next element where there appears to be a great need. Each of the chapters that follow will provide you with suggestions to enable you to develop positive qualities where there now may be a problem.

ໜ໌ ໜ໌ ໜ໌

From experience we have found that it helps if these needs are developed in sequence. Unless children feel secure, it is difficult for them to be honest with themselves and others regarding their strengths and weaknesses or their identity. Likewise, unless a child feels comfortable in his identity he is apt to have a difficult time relating to others and developing the sense of belonging. The sense of purpose and competence cannot really be developed until a child has a strong sense of the first three elements— security, identity and belonging. This may not occur until about age eight or nine. This is why we recommend that you focus on these elements in sequence. As you establish the conditions that address these elements or needs, you will enable your children to develop multiple skills and healthy attitudes, and grow in personal effectiveness and self-esteem.

ໜ໌ ໜ໌ ໜ໌

Diagnostic Checklist

The behaviors listed below can be used to indicate which social/emotional need your child probably lacks. If your child exhibits three or more symptoms under Security, refer to the suggestions for strengthening this area before focusing on the other areas. If your child exhibits less than three symptoms, move on to Identity. If your child exhibits fewer than three symptoms in this area, move on to Belonging, and then on to Purpose and Competence.

Indicators of a lack of Security

____ Exhibits numerous fears
____ Bites nails or has other nervous symptoms
____ Displays temper tantrums
____ Challenges authority
____ Ignores directions
____ Is disrespectful or defiant
____ Fails to assume personal responsibility

Indicators of a lack of Identity

____ Is overanxious to please
____ Complains about others
____ Finds it difficult to accept reality
____ Is hypersensitive
____ Needs to be at the center of attention
____ Is painfully shy
____ Brags, boasts or shows off frequently

Indicators of a lack of Belonging

____ Has few friends
____ Teases or picks on others
____ Tries to get attention from peers
____ Lacks social skills
____ Frequently in conflict with peers
____ Lacks empathy for others

Indicators of a lack of Purpose

____ Demonstrates little or no effort
____ Has to be coaxed to do homework
____ Doesn't care about work quality
____ Complains about being bored
____ Is easily discouraged
____ Asks, "Why do I have to do this?"
____ Lacks focus or personal goals

Indicators of a lack of Competence

____ Is dependent upon adults for direction
____ Believes success is just luck
____ Gives up easily
____ Is discouraged about progress
____ Seldom sees consequences for actions
____ Makes poor decisions

Summary

The process of developing desired qualities in your children rests on knowing who you are, how you've become that way, what you value, and the values you want to develop in your children. The qualities mentioned above are those most parents would like to give to their children if this were possible. We believe that they are at least as important as academic skills if not more so—but the exciting news is that they are not mutually exclusive. There is absolutely no reason why we can't have young people with outstanding academic skills who also possess those human qualities we value as well. We have found that by establishing the conditions we describe in the following chapters, you can develop those qualities as well as self-esteem, consideration for others, intellectual curiosity, tolerance and appreciation for others, self-acceptance, and a loving nature. These qualities can be developed by all children regardless of race, religion, social background, or degree of intelligence. An openness and willingness of heart is all that is required.

Chapter 2
The Role of Parents, Grandparents, and the Family

"Feelings of worth can flourish only in an atmosphere where individual differences are appreciated, mistakes are tolerated, communication is open, and rules are flexible—the kind of atmosphere that is found in a nurturing family."

Virginia Satir

ॐ ॐ ॐ

Families come in many sizes and varieties. The family of today is often very different from the traditional family of two parents with mother remaining at home to care for the children. Today, it is not uncommon for children to experience a variety of family compositions, having been the products of separation and divorce or adoption. Some are being raised by single mothers, by single fathers, by two women or by two men. In other homes, grandparents may be the designated primary caregivers helping a single teenage mother, or may simply be babysitting the kids after school. Whatever the size or composition of the family, parenting with conscious effort and plans and goals must be the focus for children.

In earlier times the extended family served as a nourishing environment for children. Grandparents were often living in the same household and provided a mediating force between children and their parents. Today, economic conditions have caused most families to move from the communities where they grew up, leaving their extended families and seeking employment elsewhere. In the year 1900, 90% of American children had close access to extended family members. By 1940, this percentage was reduced to 70%. Today it is reported that fewer than 10% of children have such access. This is why it is important that grandparents, aunts, and uncles play an active role in imparting knowledge, wisdom, and nurturing when they have the opportunity to be with children of the family.

This book aims to provide insights and suggestions for all those responsible for the care and nurturing of children, regardless of the family composition. While the comments are addressed to parents, they really apply to grandparents, other members of the extended family, and any other long-term caregivers as well.

༂༂༂

Issues related to family structure

A great deal of research has been conducted on the impact of family structure on children, specifically whether children brought up in two-parent families have a significant advantage over those brought up with single parents. Generally, children who grow up in a family with two parents have an advantage, but only if certain conditions are present. When both parents are working, for example, it has been found that many parents spend less time with their children than do those in single-parent homes. Parents in two-career families often find it difficult to "shut off" the work and fully attend to a child's needs, even when at home. Research has found that the number of hours a parent spends away from home at work is not as important as the quality of the parenting displayed when he or she is at home. Time allocation and the priority to being "fully there" is important.

In fact, it has been found that one-parent families can provide just as much support, nurturing, and self-esteem as two-parent families. In many single-parent families there is more communication with children than in two-parent families. Children who grow up in single-parent homes often demonstrate greater personal responsibility. This is likely because, in single-parent families, children often need to take on more responsibilities as a matter of necessity.

In this day and age, finding time to have a meal together is almost impossible. It seems that today 18 out of 20 families do not eat dinner together. Yet studies show the family dinner to be one of the most important priorities towards building functioning esteeming families. According to an article in the October 27, 2003, issue of *Time* magazine, sociologists in the 80s promoted structured activities to defeat juvenile delinquency and keep children safe. At the same time, education experts felt that children needed to work harder to compete in a global economy and prepare for entrance into the "best" colleges. According to William Doherty, a University of Minnesota professor of marriage and family therapy, "Adult notions of hyper-competition and over-scheduling have created a culture of parenting that's more akin to product development, and it's robbing families of time together." An August 2003 poll for the Center for a New American Dream—an organization in Tacoma Park, Maryland, that focuses on quality of life issues—revealed that although 60% of Americans felt pressure to work too much, more than 80% wished for more family time and 52% of that group would take less money to get it!

ॐ ॐ ॐ

Studies reported in the *Adolescents Journal* indicated that adolescents who initially grew up in a two-parent family but who suffered the loss of a parent are more inclined to suffer from low self-esteem, as well as have higher rates of emotional problems and/or low academic achievement. It was also found that these children had fewer close friends, tended to spend less time with friends and participated in fewer activities.

The major impact of divorce on children and their development occurs for those between the ages of nine and fourteen at the time of the marital breakdown. Even after ten years had passed, young people of that age group who had experienced divorce of their parents regarded the experience as the most stressful in their lives and 75% seemed to suffer from low self-esteem. One-third seemed to suffer from persistent emotional problems. This phenomenon has been attributed to the common feeling on the part of the children that there must have been something they could have done to prevent the separation or divorce, or that there was something about them that caused a parent to leave.

It is important, therefore, in the event of separation or divorce that both parents help a child understand that the separation or divorce was something over which the child had no control. It is also important for parents who are considering divorce to re-member that, even though breaking up the two-parent family can put stress on children, staying together can cause stress as well. There is a considerable amount of research showing long-term adverse effects on children who experience the bad mar-riages of their parents where there is frequent conflict and abuse.

੭੭ ੭੭ ੭੭

Some activities to consider:

1. Talk with your children about members of their ex-tended family and share pictures of them so they rec-ognize them.

2. Talk with your children about their family history and help them find out all they can about how your family happened to be here and where they came from origi-nally.

3. Have your children compare their family situation with others who are less fortunate. Talk about the choices and opportunities they have that others don't have.

4. Discuss the various kinds of family compositions that exist among their friends and acquaintances, and how their friends feel about their own families.

Importance of the early years

According to the brain research done in the 1980s and 90s, the first three years of life are most critical in a child's development, as it's during this time that the child's language and intelligence begin developing. This research indicated that during the child's first three years, the more hours the mother worked per week the lower the child's language development and academic achievement would be; but by the time the child was age ten, the mother's absence did not correlate with reduced development. Research has also indicated that infants and very young children who spend more than 30 hours a week in child care are far more demanding, more noncompliant, and more aggressive, than those who spend more time with the family at home. They seem to get into fights more often, bully others, and are often mean to others to get attention.

❦ ❦❦ ❦

Harvard professor Howard Gardner identified seven different forms of intelligence and indicated that these are the product of the interaction between genetic predisposition and the environment—in other words, a combination of nurture and nature. More recent studies in brain research have revealed that intellectual skills, once thought to be innate, seem instead to be very sensitive to a person's environment. Indeed, IQ can be modified up or down depending on the nature of the child's surroundings, which provide the mental stimulation that young brains need during this period of rapid neural growth. The level of intelligence can also be reduced when children are under great stress. Many young parents, mindful of these critical years and the importance of the child's environment and interaction with a nurturing adult, are opting for extended leaves from their careers after the birth of a child. In addition, many mothers, while on leave, decide not to return to full-time work, but instead to go back to work part-time or arrange to work from home. They are choosing to opt out of the push to the top. Some families also choose to make the satisfying sacrifice by simplifying their lifestyle and/or moving to less costly locations to be at home during these important formative years.

The ideal home environment should create an atmosphere that addresses six factors: challenge, freedom, respect, warmth, control, and success. Children need the challenge of exciting things to play with and to do, tasks which cause them to stretch their imagination and abilities, and freedom to explore on their own. Research shows that under those conditions and with well-defined limits and unconditional love, children will enter school well-adjusted and with a strong sense of self-acceptance.

శ్రీ శ్రీ శ్రీ

Impact of parental relationships

The nature of the relationship parents have with their children has a direct impact on how the children feel about themselves. Because children cannot view themselves directly, they know themselves primarily through the feedback and images they receive from their parents or significant others. Parents are like mirrors in which children view themselves. These pictures tend to endure even into adult life.

Fathers and mothers bring different strengths and contributions to the parenting role. These roles generally complement each other and provide love and affection to children in different ways. Basic to anything that parents do is how they relate to one another. Having a mother and father who express mutual love provides a foundation that is of great value. When parents love one another there is little chance that children will try to manipulate or use one against another. Most important, when parents love each other, the likelihood is that they will convey this atmosphere of love to their children.

Mothers play an especially important role in the child's development. Mothers who are clear about their values and priorities tend to develop children who internalize those same values and attitudes toward life. If mother values the importance of education, for example, the child will likely consider it important to do well in school. While a child's mother or caregiver generally has the greatest impact upon how a child feels about himself or herself, there is evidence that feedback from fathers is also important.

Fathers need also to realize that their responsibilities are greater than just being the provider. They play a critical role in the development of their children along with the mother. Research supports the fact that warm, caring attitudes expressed by the father toward a child closely influence the level of the child's self-esteem. When the father is attentive and loving, a child's self-esteem is typically high. This is especially true for sons. Coldness or indifference displayed by the father typically results in low self-esteem in either boys or girls. Persistent criticism and conflict typically result in feelings of hopelessness, low self-esteem, lack of motivation, and criticism of others. However, the odd thing is that indifference or inattention is even more damaging to self-esteem and motivation than criticism.

*"Why would you want to talk to my father?
He's just like me, only bigger."*

The role of fathers during periods of adolescence is especially important. When fathers are actively involved in their son's lives, the boys turn out to be less aggressive, less overly competitive and better adjusted. On the other hand, lack of interest or absence of a father has been linked to diminished self-esteem, delinquency, violence, crime, gang membership, and poor academic achievement. In the case of girls, the absence of attention from fathers is often compensated for by girls seeking the attention of older boys.

The amount of communication and interaction between parents and their children also affects how children feel about themselves. Where there are high levels of positive interaction, children generally have positive feelings about themselves. Conversely the absence of communication or reduced levels of interaction between parents and their children contributes to low self-esteem. This interaction is especially important as children reach adolescence.

How parents react in times of crisis, their outlook on life, their values, and beliefs, all have a great bearing on how children develop, what they value, and how they feel about themselves. The ways in which parents live out their lives create the patterns for their children's lives, for children learn through example and experience.

There is evidence that parents with high self-esteem tend to raise children with high self-esteem, while parents with low self-esteem tend to raise children with low self-esteem. For this reason we have included a chapter at the end of this book with suggestions for parents, grandparents, and other caregivers as to what you might do to foster your own self-esteem so that you can serve as a better model for your child.

ᢒᢒ ᢒᢒ ᢒᢒ

Special role of grandparents

Today, grandparents are playing a new role in children's lives. Many are finding themselves in the parenting role. This means they can also play a dual role as caregivers and grandparents, and both roles are important. There are four services grandparents can provide:

1. Grandparents typically provide unconditional love for their grandchildren. It is almost as if their grandchildren can do no wrong. Everything the grandchild does is "wonderful!" so the grandchild receives lots of what is sometimes referred to as "marshmallow praise." This is the kind of praise that is rarely specific but just exudes lots of love.

2. Grandparents are great listeners. They have more time to listen than most parents, who are usually unavailable working or just busy with the demands of life for a young family. They have time to tell stories and play games with their grandchildren, so the children get valuable attention that reflects how important they are.

3. Grandparents typically have strong values that they convey to children. These help shape children's personalities and the choices they make.

4. Grandparents can often serve as a mediating force for parents when they are upset with their children. Grandparents usually have a way of putting things into perspective and reminding parents of when they were children doing the same thing. They can thus speak from the voice of experience and reason.

"My grandpa went to school when blackboards were really black."

It is unfortunate that not all children have the opportunity to interact with their grandparents on a regular basis. This is a great loss for many children, because grandparents perform these unique roles even when they don't live with their grandchildren. However, even with less frequent contact, grandparents can still make a significant impact when it is possible and practical.

A grandparent who takes on the role as parent and primary caregiver must make both physical and psychological adjustments. First, parenting requires a great expenditure of energy and stamina just as the infirmities of age begin to hit. Stress also takes its toll. A recent study by Harvard University researchers found a greater risk of heart disease among women who care for their grandchildren. Author of the study Summin Lee says, "We hypothesize that stress may be the main reason, but we also think that grandmothers may have less time or opportunity to engage in their own self-care—like regular checkups, preventive care, or getting enough sleep or exercise."

$$\mathit{\ж\ \ж\ \ж}$$

Sometimes, psychological adjustments must also take place. Grandparents may resent the fact that they have had to take on this role and feel they have already done their parenting and would rather relax and enjoy their own life. They may also wonder if they can do a good job. Obviously (they may reason) the parent of the child, whom they parented, didn't turn out too well, or at least not well enough to be a good parent! In such situations, grandparents need make certain that this resentment isn't taken out on their grandchildren.

If grandparents are unavailable, some parents have found it helpful to find neighbors, friends or other members of the extended family to take on the more traditional grandparent role so the child has those benefits. It is wise for the family to cultivate friends or members of the extended family who develop close relationships with the children in the family. Unforeseen accidents or illness can sometimes rob children of one or both parents. Having a close relationship with an adult who might serve as a surrogate parent can then be extremely important. It is wise to establish such a relationship before anything occurs, for children have sometimes resented other adults who have tried to assume that role after parental loss, believing the new adult is just trying to move in to replace their parent.

Some activities to consider:

1. Share with your children the family tree and have them trace the geographical locations where your family lived up to their birth.

2. Identify individuals who might serve as surrogate parents in the event that something might happen to you and encourage these individuals to have a close relationship with your children.

3. Discuss with your children the advantages and disadvantages of growing up at the time of their parents or grandparents versus growing up at the present time.

4. Have the children's grandparents teach them how to prepare one of the children's favorite dishes.

Parenting styles

Research has shown that the pattern of child-rearing or parenting style greatly influences the attitudes children develop towards themselves and towards authority figures. Leon Canerot in his excellent book *Tips on Parenting Strategies* says "How we raise our children is to a large extent based on what comes 'naturally' to us." What comes naturally to you may be the way you were parented. When you were growing up, perhaps you swore to yourself that you would always answer your child's questions with reasonable and logical replies, never lose your temper, and never reply as your mother did, "Because I told you so!" When put to the test as a parent, however, you may hear those very words coming from your mouth, although you swear it's your mother's voice saying ... "Because I told you so."

Many parents are unsure how strict to be, or they vacillate between being overly permissive and being overly strict. Neither strictness nor permissiveness is the answer, as either extreme is apt to result in problems as children mature. It is important, however, that parents be authoritative. Authoritative means that the parent(s) can set limits which are age-appropriate and are based on natural and logical consequences, yet which at the same time demonstrate warmth and nurturing. This balance brings social reality into the home and the life of the child.

Author Leon Canerot described four types of parenting styles:

Chairman/Chairperson:

The chairman is obviously in charge but the child is a member of the board and power is shared. The relationship is one of mutual respect and cooperation. The chairman is the leader and entitled to make final and big decisions, but the child has input in the decision-making process and can make choices within clearly defined limits. There is balance between responsibility and freedom that both empowers and yet develops self-discipline, self-control, and self-esteem. This parenting style provides the support and structure necessary for children to realize fully their uniqueness and come to know their true selves. They feel empowered by trusting themselves, others, and the future.

Commander:

The commander is the authoritarian or dictator style. His/her word is the law. There is no discussion, no compromise, and usually very little conversation. The structure is rigid and is used for control and power, both of which are in the hands of the parents. Most issues are fairly black-and-white and rules are ironclad and dogmatic. Emotions are not openly expressed and/or encouraged. The shortcomings of this style are pretty obvious, but the advantage is that the child knows what is expected and usually knows the consequences of not meeting those expectations. However, the outcome of such families is that they tend to raise children who know what to think but not how to think or feel, and who lack a sense of a true self.

"Why didn't his mother just yank back the covers and threaten him like you do?

Counselor:

This is the psychologist/analyst who talks and talks and looks for deeper reasons for a particular behavior and tries to persuade the child to his/her point of view. The child often has unlimited choices and often attempts to do the same—to persuade/manipulate to his/her point of view to gain his/her objective. Sometimes counseling and guidance are certainly appropriate and desirable, but with the counselor-type parent it usually results in constant negotiating. Because limits and standards are often vague, the choices are often overwhelming. Children raised in such an environment tend to confuse the roles of adult and child, believing that they have equal power in the decision-making process. A major concern is that such children may develop difficulty interacting with adult authority.

The Peer Parent:

This is the parent type who wants to be the friend and on equal footing when it comes to decision making. He or she wants to "buddy" with the child and the child's friends, and encourages them to call him or her by first name. When carried to extreme, the parent (usually the mom) tries to dress in clothes more appropriate for the child. He/she wants to share secrets, sometimes taking sides against the other parent. There is an absence of structure. In fact, the need for structure may not even be acknowledged or understood. There are few if any routines or limits. This parent has an anxious, pleasing, permissive attitude; the child may feel he/she has *carte blanche* with respect to behavior. "I can do anything I want to do" usually translates into "nobody cares." The child develops little respect for the parent as an adult. This parent is heavily involved with the child's activities; the child has no separation from the parent and no practice in developing self-control and independent thinking.

ණ ඡ ණ

In one of her parenting classes, Marilyn asked the parents to group themselves according to the four parenting styles. After discussing the four styles, parents in the class were asked to gather together by the type of parenting they had experienced. They were then asked to go back in time to remember incidents that had occurred in their lives and how it felt to be "parented" in that way. The discussion became lively and animated and even heated with one parent shouting, "I haven't spoken to my mother since that day!" We certainly don't want to incite anger or hostility, but we do want you and your partner to consider your own childhood and how you were parented so that you can develop your own parenting style. If you consider the way you were parented to have been positive and valuable for the most part, consciously refer to it when you need to keep things in perspective or make parenting decisions. If it was not positive and valuable, remember how it felt and although it might come naturally, make a conscious effort to change the way you parent your own children. One mother who had experienced an abusive parenting style said, "I am parenting the way I wish I had been parented!"

Research shows that the style we refer to as the Chairman or Chairperson is most effective in raising responsible, resilient children. We would also emphasize the importance of modeling and mentoring. Children emulate and remember what we do more often than what we say!

Refrigerators hold pictures and appointment notices. Perhaps they are also good places to post "Refrigerator Rules To Remember."

Rule One: Always Convey Caring.
Rule Two: Be an M and M parent—remember
to model and mentor!

ஐ ஐ ஐ

Some activities to consider:

1. Discuss with your spouse or partner the parenting style of each of your parents and the degree to which you model that same style.

2. Gather old clothes, hats, glasses and other items that could be used for your child as costumes to play "mother or father" or other roles.

3. Make a family pact to try not to push each other's buttons or bug other members of the family.

4. Create with your family a list of Children's Rights and Parents' Rights that will serve as a basis for agreement about protecting each other's rights within the family.

The impact of abuse

A few words need to be said regarding abuse, the subject most families find difficult to talk about. A great deal of concern has been expressed, and for good reason, regarding the abuse of children. Even very young children under the age of three are sensitive to clues they receive from their parents. When they are subjected to an environment where there is anarchy or conflict, they tend to become insecure and suffer in terms of esteem.

There is clear evidence that physical, emotional, or sexual abuse can have a devastating effect on children. At least 50% of the victims or witnesses to abuse in the home suffer from low self-esteem. The impact of such abuse often has a lasting effect through adolescence and into adulthood. A high percentage of these children never fully recover. Such children are ten times more likely to become either abusers or victims of abuse later on. Emotional abuse, including yelling, constantly criticizing, calling the child embarrassing names, or emotional rejection, can be even more psychologically damaging than physical abuse.

♪ ♪ ♪

Long-term studies of children who were abused found that, after five years, they still suffered from low self-esteem, depression, or behavioral dysfunction. Abuse has been found to be a primary reason juvenile girls run away from home and go into prostitution. The negative identity and low self-esteem as a result of negative home experiences can thus cause adolescents to take drastic steps to escape, either physically or emotionally by means of drugs or alcohol. It's for this reason that schools and other authorities are required to report any suspected form of home-abuse of children. Most abuse occurs within the family by those who should be the child's protector! Thus, parents must do everything they can to be advocates for their child and alert to any kind of abuse from sources inside or outside of the family.

Summary

The structure of the family is not the important issue in parenting. Single-parent families can be just as effective as two-parent families since it depends upon the quality of time children spend with their parents that makes the difference. Grandparents have a special role they can play, whether they are the primary caregivers or not. As a parent you have a choice in how you want to relate to your children. Become the kind of parent you consciously choose to be, make the time you spend with your children valuable, and develop a loving relationship with them. The home environment is the single greatest determinant of how children feel about themselves and the attitudes they develop. You, yourself, play the major role in this process. Become that M and M parent!

Chapter 3
Key #1: Creating a Sense of Security

"Only a child who feels safe dares to grow forward in a healthy fashion. His safety needs must be gratified to begin with."

Abraham Maslow

❧ ❧ ❧

The first basic need of parenting is to create feelings of security in children. A great deal has been written recently regarding the increased level of anxiety, stress, and nervousness exhibited by children today. More children are undergoing treatment for stress disorders, ulcers, nervous stomachs, and hyperactivity than ever before. In order for children to function most effectively, they need to feel secure enough to be relatively free from extreme worries and stress. Those children who lack feelings of security are inclined to exhibit nervous symptoms and anxiety; they are typically reluctant to make decisions for themselves so are easily misled by their peers. They are apt to test out authority and the rules they are expected to follow, and they tend not to feel responsible for their actions but blame others for their problems.

The object of the sense of security is to enable children to feel secure enough to take responsibility for themselves and to begin to take on challenges. By creating an environment that fosters security, you, as a parent, can do a great deal to reduce stress, insecurity, and worries. This practice begins with the foundation of positive parenting, unconditional love, and letting your children know how much you care about them. Create a home environment characterized by warmth, trust and respect. Make it a safe refuge, both physically and emotionally for children. That is the foundation of security for children. We hope to help provide suggestions so that your family problems can be solved, conflicts resolved, feelings expressed, roles explored, and risks taken.

Feelings of security come from knowing what to expect, feeling safe and protected, being able to trust others, and having the ability to anticipate what is likely to happen in situations. Children with a good sense of security are more willing to take initiative when they enter new situations and are better able to apply themselves to the tasks at hand. They feel free to ask questions, express opinions, and participate with others in new experiences. With feelings of security children are more apt to take responsibility for themselves and their actions.

ॐ ॐ ॐ

General guidelines for discipline

Establishing a framework and strategies for effective discipline is an important step in parenting with purpose. The word "discipline" often implies following one's own or an outside authority, like a parent. It usually involves coercive or forced compliance, rewards, and punishments. However, the root word of "discipline" is "disciple," which originally meant "joyful follower." The most effective discipline results from the child having a joyful relationship with a parent or adult.

We include discipline in the context of security because to develop a sense of security, children need to know what is expected of them, and they need to be able to trust the adults in their lives. As a parent, your actions should be consistent with your promises. When you interact with your child in a predictable fashion your child learns to trust your behavior. Sharing promises, fulfilling agreements, sticking to schedules, and keeping your child's confidence deepens this trust.

Most parents have questions about how to discipline their children. The primary guideline is: (Refrigerator Rule #1) Always Convey Caring! Children need to know that they are loved by you, no matter what—even when they create a mess or get into trouble. The structure you provide and how you implement it should serve to make them feel more secure, not more anxious and nervous for fear of punishment.

The rules should be broad enough to serve as general guidelines for behavior, because the goal of discipline is self-discipline. Children should be able to apply that same guideline when they find themselves in a new situation. For example, one such standard might be "We only use the property of others with permission." This then includes mother's clothes or dad's tools. It also establishes a basis for school rules later on and the avoidance of being accused of stealing. Another standard might be "We treat others and their property with respect." This can then be applied to siblings, neighbors, and schoolmates.

❧ ❧ ❧

Whenever possible, state standards in positive rather than negative terms. Children following the standards know they're pleasing you and develop positive self-images. When standards are set in terms of what not to do, it is not as effective as stating the behavior desired. A negative message such as "Don't get in the cookie jar" is liable to conjure up images of cookies rather than focusing on what you want your child to do. A better message might be "When you have finished your lunch I will get you a cookie." Using "I" messages is one way to do this. Here are some "I" messages that are more effective than negative statements for they clarify what is desired or needed:

"I need you to be quiet when I am on the telephone."
"It helps me when you close the door quietly."
"I really like it when you pick up your toys."

When children understand what is expected and the standards are clear to them it adds to their feelings of control and significance.

Establishing structure and behavioral expectations

It is important that you clearly describe the type of behavior you expect. Children actually feel more secure when there is structure in their lives, with clear limits, established routines and when they know exactly what is expected. Knowing what you consider to be acceptable and unacceptable behavior builds security. Naturally, it is important that the standards you set be age-appropriate. This is sometimes difficult when you have more than one child, for what is appropriate for one may not be reasonable for another, especially a younger child. For example, it may be reasonable to expect a child of four or five to be responsible for keeping his bed made and room clean. However, a younger brother or sister can learn to be responsible by picking up toys after play-time.

When setting expectations, it's important that adults responsible for the child agree upon what will be considered acceptable and not acceptable behavior, so these standards can be consistently enforced. Expectations and limits should be negotiated and adjusted from time to time as children mature and become more responsible. One way in which Bob did this as a parent was to sit down whenever the child had a birthday to reestablish expectations, job responsibilities, and privileges. His children usually wanted to negotiate one additional privilege, such as being able to go to the store by themselves or stay up 30 minutes later. Together they negotiated one additional responsibility that they might be expected to take on, reinforcing the fact that additional privileges also carried with them additional responsibilities. This negotiation process was something that always made birthdays special, and it served as an official way to recognize that the children were growing up and becoming more responsible.

Routines, another important form of structure, add to children's sense of security. It helps to have established routines for getting ready for bed or school, handling chores, and studying. When set and followed on a daily basis, routines eliminate the need for constant reminding and the resulting resentment on the part of children. It also makes it easier for children to follow the same routine each day and gives them a feeling of being responsible and in control of their lives.

Some activities to consider:

1. Help your very young child memorize his or her full name, address, and telephone number.

2. Establish routines for your children for getting ready for school, meal time, doing schoolwork, and getting ready for school.

3. Review your expectations of your children with respect to chores, bedtime procedure, doing schoolwork, feeding pets, and other responsibilities. Set up a chart to monitor their chores.

4. Talk about how the rules you have in your home may be similar or different from those in other homes they might visit or in the classroom at school.

"I can't come to school today because I have a barking cough. Wanna hear it?"

Your children, especially young children, want to please you as their parent. If they understand "The Rules" and the expectations you have for them as well as the positive and negative consequences of keeping or breaking the rules, preventive discipline will be in place. Whenever possible, include your children in setting the rules and consequences, both positive and negative. For example, you might say, "We need to have an agreement regarding when you are to get ready for bed. Lights should be out at 9:00. Do you want time to read in bed before then or go right to bed?" "What should be the consequence if you are not in bed ready for lights out at 9:00?" If you negotiate with them to reach a mutual agreement, children are usually more responsible in following through than if you merely issue an order.

The focus of any disciplinary action should be to teach or train the child in proper behavior, not to inflict punishment. Take as much time as necessary to explain or demonstrate to your child exactly what is expected, and even have the child go through the process several times so that there is no question about the desired outcome. When not implemented correctly, refer to the standard you explained or demonstrated and revisit it. This is the easiest form of discipline.

ଚତ ଚତ ଚତ

Following the rules responsibly should also carry positive consequences. As children demonstrate responsible behavior, they should be offered additional privileges and freedom. For example, completing chores without whining and complaining might earn a child a day off from a particularly disliked chore. Adhering to curfew might mean a later night on occasion or more opportunities to socialize with friends. One mother reported that she had trouble getting her children ready for school in time to catch the bus. She set up a "Surprise Can" on the breakfast table that contained slips of paper. Each slip contained a special reward such as getting to choose what they wanted for dinner, having the last piece of chocolate cake in their lunch, or getting to select the video to watch that evening. Only those children who arrived at the breakfast table on time got to pull a slip from the can. Later, the can was put there only occasionally rather than every day. She reported that it solved the problem.

Some activities to consider:

1. Transferring responsibility from parent to child is a continuum as children begin to take on more and more responsibility for themselves. Chart your children's responsibilities and encourage them to take on more as you feel they are able.

2. Teach your child how to take care of his/her own needs as early as possible, e.g. getting dressed by himself, making her own sandwich, tying his shoes, and picking up her room.

3. Discuss what your family would be like if you had no rules and no enforcement of expectations.

4. Develop a plan with your family to handle emergencies. Talk about what your children should do in different kinds of emergencies, what they might wish to take with them if you have time, where you might meet, a common person to contact, where essential equipment is stored and how to use it. Have a practice session.

Whenever you are able to anticipate a problem, it helps to give the child a choice by discussing the consequences that are likely to take place if failure should occur. For example, if toys are not picked up as asked or expected, the agreement might be to have them removed from use for a period of time. When consequences have been set out ahead of time, you can reinforce the fact that the child had the choice of following the rule or assuming the penalty. This procedure helps to foster a sense of responsibility and personal power. The important goal is to make certain such agreements are enforced consistently. When they're not, children are apt to become anxious, confused, or resentful, and as they grow older they can become skillful at focusing on what they can get away with, especially when two or more adults are involved.

The task of enforcing rules in a single-parent household is easier in some respects, because it may avoid such conflicts. When children need to interact with several different adults such as babysitters or care-center personnel, consistent enforcement becomes more difficult. For this reason both single- and two-career parents should make certain that all adults responsible for the child or children understand the standards of behavior set at home and strive to be consistent in their expectations and enforcement.

When two parents have different standards or lack consistency in enforcement, a child will learn how to work one adult against the other. Typical threats such as "Do you want me to tell your mother?" or "Wait until your father gets home" encourage children to become adept at pleading to avoid punishment rather than to accept responsibility for their own behavior. This is also true when divorced parents have two different sets of expectations and approaches to discipline. Every effort should be made to reach agreement between the adults involved.

ॐ ॐ ॐ

An important guideline for discipline is never to discipline in anger—yours or your children's. It is important to be firm about not accepting inappropriate behavior, making it clear that such behavior must stop. At the same time, you need to deal with your children in a caring, supportive way to help them express their anger. Usually the time to talk about misbehavior is not when the problem is occurring but later, when everyone has calmed down and can respond rationally.

One strategy for dealing with misbehavior when emotions are high is to establish a pattern of "time out" until emotions calm down to avoid escalation. "Time out" is most effective when the child goes to a place where he or she is not seen or heard and can be by himself or herself. Sending the child to his or her room is sometimes appropriate, but that may not be seen as a punishment when there are lots of pleasant things to do there. It's also probably not desirable to have the child associate the bedroom with punishment. Having your child sit on the floor or at the dining room table with nothing to do for a short while is often more effective. If he is to remain there for a period of minutes, only count the minutes when the child is in full compliance rather than fussing or screaming. It is also not such a bad idea for you, as the parent, to request "time out" for yourself if you need time to regain your composure and not take action when you are full of anger or hostility.

॰ॐ ॐ ॐ

Another guideline when disciplining a child is first to express your regret or sorrow at having to follow up on consequences because of the child's misbehavior. Always try to reinforce your love for the child and separate it from your concern about the behavior itself, though this can be difficult at times. It may help to express empathy for the unhappy feelings the child may be experiencing, but that you are only following up on the consequence of his or her choice not to follow directions.

॰ॐ ॐ ॐ

It's helpful to directly relate the consequence to the misbehavior. If a child creates a mess the consequence should carry with it the responsibility for cleaning it up. Not coming to dinner when dinner is ready may result in having to eat a cold dinner. It is easier to use consequences when certain privileges have been established for following the rules or procedures. Then it becomes a simple matter of losing the privilege, which might be watching TV, using the telephone, going to a friend's house, or asking for a ride.

The consequences established should be reasonable and proportionate to the misbehavior. The purpose of this follow-up is to teach your children correct behavior, not to inflict punishment to make them suffer. Children are generally more highly motivated to respond to privileges than they are to avoid punishments. Punishments are more apt to be resented than natural consequences because punishments typically are not related to the misbehavior. Often the punishment that is administered is not done respectfully, but instead is punitive and results in hostility and antagonism.

As children get older, an effective strategy is to establish a system whereby they can monitor their own behavior. For example, when Bob's daughter wished to go out at night he and she would agree on the return time. The alarm clock would then be set for that time. His daughter's job was to get home in time to shut off the alarm clock before it went off. If the alarm sounded, the consequence was that she had to come in 30 minutes earlier next time. Through self-monitoring, feelings of personal responsibility were reinforced rather than her resenting having a parent monitor her behavior.

One of the most highly prized rewards for most children is extra time with a parent—an opportunity to go shopping together, see a movie together, bake a cake together, go fishing together, or go on a picnic. Some parents like to give rewards for good behavior with money or material items like toys, but establishing consequences for choices and connecting the cause and effect is much more meaningful and helpful in establishing self-discipline.

Some activities to consider:

1. Have your child make a list of the rewards that would really motivate him or her. Use this list as a basis for rewarding behaviors that are really important to you.

2. Discuss with your children why parents need to be firm about enforcing rules and standards of behavior, why this is important, and where your children may feel they are unrealistic or unreasonable.

3. Establish the practice of putting clothes, games, or other belongings away for a while in a "Safe Deposit Box" for a week as a consequence of not putting them where they should be.

4. Take one area where you would like your children to take greater personal responsibility, and reach agreement on what would be an appropriate natural consequence for failing to take responsibility.

Why children misbehave

Every parent has to deal on occasion with the problem of a misbehaving child. Children normally want to please their parents, but when they don't, you need to ask yourself why. When your child is acting up, the first thing you need to do is to step back, relax, and listen to what your child seems to be communicating. It is not the time to escalate the problem by yelling at your child or taking steps you might not take at a more rational moment. It is important that you come up with a hypothesis as to what your misbehaving child is trying to convey to you. Since most young children lack the verbal skills or the personal awareness to understand their underlying feelings and motivation, you need to become a detective, so to speak, to guess what the problem is. This is important because we can respond in ways that make the problem worse unless we have some idea as to what the child is trying to communicate. There seem to be four common explanations as to why children misbehave:

1. Seeking to gain attention

2. Looking to gain power

3. Engaging in revengeful behavior

4. Avoiding failure or embarrassment

Seeking to gain attention

Children often seek attention from their parents when they feel a lack of recognition or love. When they want your attention there are multiple ways that they can find to "bug" you or to gain your attention in ways you don't appreciate. It might be by whining, complaining, not following through on their responsibilities, picking on siblings, etc. This may be due to the fact that you have been too busy for them or that other siblings, such as a new baby, have received more attention than they. An easy solution is to express your insights regarding the problem to the child and find some acceptable way in which the child can gain your attention. If we choose to isolate the child or become angry because of his or her misbehavior, we may just make the problem worse. An effective way to head off the problem is to create ways by which your child can obtain positive attention, perhaps by having him sit next to you, by your sitting down to listen to whatever she wishes to talk about, or by asking him or her to help you.

Looking to gain power

Second, most children test limits and the extent of their power or authority with their parents. This is the basis for "the terrible twos" for young children and for many of the problems with adolescents. Children don't always act out their need for power in aggressive ways. They may engage in power struggles by being passive rather than by acting out. They may "forget" to do things, act in a lazy manner, or just not comply with requests. Others may actually act out through temper tantrums, may become sassy, or may respond in a confronting or defiant manner. (It seems as if this often occurs when others are around as in a grocery store, because children know it is more difficult for parents to respond under those circumstances.) Parents can engage in power struggles with their children and win some of the time, but then later find they are the recipients of revengeful behavior that stems from resentment. Thus it is advisable to try to distract the child or defuse the situation to avoid getting into a power struggle with your child whenever possible.

꘎ꘚ꘎ꘚꘚ

It is important not to put up with disrespectful or violent behavior, but we don't need to prove our power or emphasize "blind obedience." One effective way of dealing with children who seem to be seeking power is to avoid a confrontation if at all possible by removing yourself from it, and then come back and discuss it later when things are calmer. Other strategies include distracting the child or defusing the situation by moving on to another setting. Another strategy is to review with your child the limits, agreements, or procedures that have been laid out earlier and the reason why those were established and the importance of keeping those standards. In some cases setting up a small reward for behaving in ways agreed upon is effective.

Some might advocate spanking a child for disrespectful behavior, but for several reasons this is not a form of punishment which we recommend. First, whenever possible it should be your intention to honor the child's dignity and right to feel safe. Hence, using physical punishment would violate that objective. Second, when we take our frustrations out on a child it can easily result in serious injury or abuse. Third, when physical punishment is used it tends to destroy your relationship with the child, causing resentment, hate, fear and insecurity rather than mutual respect and love. This is especially true for children of school age. Again, disrespectful behavior should not be allowed to go unchecked, but try to seek a consequence other than physical spanking.

ॐ ॐ ॐ

Engaging in revengeful behavior

Another reason for children's misbehavior is an attempt on their part to seek revenge or retaliation for what they perceive as an injustice. They may sulk, scowl or lash out. They can seem to be on edge as if they are apt to explode at any time at the slightest provocation. They often begin by trying to hurt your feelings, stating that they don't love you anymore. Such behavior may not even have been the result of anything you have done, but something that happened at school. Children seeking revenge or retaliation typically display hurt as well as anger. Our initial reaction is to respond with anger, frustration, or hurt, but that is only likely to escalate the problem. We need to remember that children in this situation are coming from hurt, so it helps to reinforce a caring relationship and reflect your perception that they feel hurt and are angry. Teach them how they can express their hurt appropriately and invite them to talk about it with you.

ॐ ॐ ॐ

Avoiding the possibility of failure or embarrassment

The fourth type of misbehavior stems from attempts to avoid embarrassment or perceived failure. The child feels more secure if she acts incapable so others will not expect so much from her. For example, this might occur if your child is forced to compete in some way and she doesn't feel she has a chance to succeed. It can also occur if you were to ask your child to sing or perform in front of peers or other adults where he might suffer embarrassment. In such a situation the child is apt to respond by acting up and refusing to do what he is asked.

The incident mentioned earlier when Bob resented having to entertain relatives at holiday times is one such example. That was the time when he and his cousins hid in the attic so they wouldn't have to perform, much to the consternation of their parents. Fortunately, the parents sat down and asked what the children were thinking and why they were being so resistant. After they had a chance to talk, the children explained their position and that became the end of holiday performances. If the parents had dealt only with the defiance and used adult power to force the issue it would likely have fostered revengeful or retaliating attitudes. (Fortunately, his cousins did not quit performing, as they both ended up playing with major symphony orchestras, often as soloists.)

When we want to modify children's behavior we need to look at the optional ways in which we might respond, and the reason for the child's misbehavior, rather than just issuing a punishment. In this way we are more apt to achieve positive interactions with our children and help them develop self-discipline.

*"His teacher gives him too much homework.
I've gained five pounds since school started."*

Why home chores are important

Children gain feelings of self-esteem when they learn from an early age about handling responsibilities. It is sometimes easier for adults to handle tasks than to require children to do those chores. However, having responsibilities can be a valuable learning experience for them. Studies show that those children who have been assigned and completed chores while they were growing up became more responsible adults, had happier marriages, held jobs longer, and were five times less apt to be arrested for crimes.

Children especially feel good about themselves when a parent or adult has enough faith in them to ask them to handle an important task. It conveys a sense of trust and enhances motivation. They basically want to be helpful. This is especially true for activities that contribute to the welfare of those in their family or community.

ॐ ॐ ॐ

It also helps to reinforce the contribution children make to the welfare of others, emphasizing that you need their help to be able to carry out your functions as a parent. For example, you might say, "It really helps when you put your clothes in the hamper to be washed. Then I don't have to decide which are dirty and which are clean."

ॐ ॐ ॐ

Chores that are assigned should be appropriate to the age level of the child, but even pre-school children begin to feel more grown up when they can learn to set the table before a meal. Taking care of pets can be an excellent way to begin handling responsibilities, along with keeping their room reasonably well picked up. When there are several children in the family, it helps to sometimes rotate the chores so one child is not always stuck with the same tasks. It also makes it easier when everyone in the family is doing chores at the same time rather than having to force children to do their chores when everyone else is enjoying a TV program.

In assigning tasks, it is helpful to spell out when the task is to be completed, how it is to be done, and what it should look like when finished. Having a designated time to do the chore, such as homework for example, makes it easier to enforce and builds self-responsibility when the child begins to take on the chore without being reminded. You may even find it helpful to perform the task with her the first few times. By making certain that your child clearly understands how and when the task is to be completed, you can avoid problems later.

Some children are motivated when there is a chart of chores or things that need to be done. In this way children can check off the chores or put a star next to their names when the assigned chores have been done. Sometimes a reward such as being able to decide what they want for dinner at the end of the week serves as an incentive to complete their chores each day. Some find that the reward of an allowance serves as a good motivation device. Most parents find that it is necessary to try new strategies when old ones no longer serve their purposes. Changing reward strategies helps to remind your children how much they have grown and how much more responsibility they have assumed. Ultimately, children should reach the stage when no incentives are necessary and doing chores just becomes a routine—simply because they are members of a family.

Some activities to consider:

1. Expect your child to do some of the chores at home, including care of his/or her room and belongings. Give allowance or compensation only for those things the child does for the rest of the family.

2. Talk with your children about what "responsibility" means. Discuss how it applies to home chores.

3. Have your children evaluate the degree to which they take responsibility for themselves with respect to such things as chores, cleanliness, promptness, homework, money, eating, etc. Have them identify those areas in which they already accept responsibility for themselves and those areas where it is especially difficult for them to be responsible.

4. Help your young child organize toys by choosing a place for each toy. Give your child a chance to be involved in decision making by asking him where he would like to keep each toy. Then label containers with pictures of what belongs inside.

Give children choices

Children need to feel that they have a choice in such matters as what to wear, where to go, what to do, and what to say. By giving them choices we also prepare them for independent, responsible decision making. This takes time and training. It also helps when they are treated with respect and the choice is stated in terms of a preference. A general guideline is to limit the number of choices to the age of the child. Thus, a child two years of age should not be given more than two choices, or a child of three not more than three choices.

When children make an independent choice, it is often a good practice on occasion to have them evaluate the decision so that they can learn to make a more appropriate choice the next time. Adolescents often like to try out new roles and experiences. It is important for them to be able to do so in a safe environment while understanding the possible consequences of their behaviors and actions. Whenever possible, parents need to do what they can to provide the support needed to increase the child's chances of success. However, it is critical that you not step in to save them from taking risks or bail them out when they get into difficulty. Children need to learn to manage on their own as much as they possibly can without adult intervention, for this is how they develop confidence in their abilities.

In order for children to feel comfortable in making choices and taking risks, they need to feel they can trust you and your judgment. This is especially important when they are facing new situations, trying a new skill, or struggling to learn. They need to feel comfortable enough to try for success and to risk failure. Let them know when you feel you, yourself, are taking a risk so that they see that it is a natural experience. Talk with them about the worst thing that could happen to them as a result of taking that risk. Doing so will help them anticipate the possibilities, develop a plan to address the situation, lessen the possibility of failure, and help them decide if the risk is worth taking. If they could handle the consequence of not succeeding then it might be worth taking that risk.

ঞ্চ ঞ্চ ঞ্চ

One mother reported that her son and a friend had asked if they could take their paint guns to the public park to play. She gave her permission to go, but failed to have them evaluate the conditions under which it would be appropriate to use their paint guns. When their paint balls ended up splattering some of the buildings in the area, the boys were arrested and required to appear before a judge for defacing property. The mother, being conscientious, felt she was responsible since she permitted them to go. She considered taking the blame herself and excusing the boys. However, had she done so, the boys might have learned from this experience to shift the blame onto someone else next time rather than learn to be more responsible in their use of the paint guns. Consequently, both she and the boys went before the judge, as she felt they shared in the responsibility for what happened.

∞ ∞ ∞

Help children deal with fears and anxieties

Family changes and crises tend to create anxieties in children because they feel personally threatened, not knowing what to expect. Those who have experienced their parents' separation or divorce frequently feel they might be abandoned or suddenly unloved. Many children have anxiety over losing a parent because one of their playmates or schoolmates had this happen. Children need to understand that situations may change but most of the familiar aspects of their lives will not be affected. Whenever changes in family conditions, living arrangements, employment, or school attendance can be anticipated, explain to your child what is to take place and what plans are being made.

Most children also have fears—fear of the dark, fear of animals, fear of strangers, fear of being embarrassed or making a fool of themselves so that others will laugh at them. Take time to discuss your child's fears from time to time and don't discount or belittle these fears. The fears may seem trivial to you, but to children these fears can be frightening. Take time to talk with your children about their fears in ways that enable them to deal with those fears. Enable your children to believe that they can be in control and deal with their anxieties rather than be controlled by them.

One helpful technique is to have your child list all the things he fears might happen. Then brainstorm with him ways he might deal with those situations if they should occur. Such situations might include how to deal with a fire in the house, what to do if he feels lost, or what to do if he can't get into the house. The child who is prepared ahead of time for such situations is less apt to feel a sense of anxiety and fear whenever in those situations.

Some activities to consider:

1. Have your child decorate a shoe box labeled "Worry Box." Whenever there is something she is worried about, have her write it out and put it in the shoe box. At the end of the week set aside some "Worry Time" to deal with these worries.

2. Have your child discuss some of the things he fears or worries about and whether or not these areas of concern are real or imagined.

3. Share with your children the fears that you use to have that no longer bother you. Try to recall how you overcame those fears.

Summary

The objective in fostering a sense of security is to convey to children the feeling that their family is a safe harbor, a place of physical and emotional safety. Fears and anxieties are reduced and trust is developed as children learn to anticipate situations and explore possible solutions. Within the family, children will feel secure because they feel loved and protected, are treated with respect, given choices and opportunities for expression and self development, and have a clear understanding of parental expectations. They will assume responsibilities as contributing members of the family and accept control of their own behaviors and actions with loving discipline that provides guidelines and consequences. The gradual growth toward an internal sense of control will enable them to act independently and responsibly and with the self-esteem necessary for resiliency in life.

ھۄ۔ ۞ ھۄ۔

Chapter 4
Key #2: Strengthening the Sense of Identity

*"I believe every person carries a complex self inside of themselves.
It is an invisible organ. It is our identity. All our feelings,
need for expression, our fears, the conscious and unconscious
are related to that identity and this is what determines our actions."*

Anna-Marie Roeper

ॐ ॐ ॐ

The second key is to have your child develop positive feelings about himself. This is a basic need all children have. Most parents would like to see in their children qualities like empathy, caring, consideration, compassion, and respect for others. These qualities are generally considered to be essential in order to achieve success in so many professions and certainly in those that involve helping or serving others. Such qualities are normally the result of a positive self-image or identity, reflecting the positive feelings and pride individuals feel about themselves. Children act in ways that are consistent with how they see themselves and the expectations they believe others have of them. If they have negative feelings about themselves, there is a natural tendency for them to relate to others in negative rather than positive ways. Developing a positive sense of identity or self-concept should therefore be one of your purposes in parenting.

The child who sees himself or herself as unattractive will act in ways that are consistent with that self-concept. A boy who is referred to as a bully is quite likely to act like a bully because that is what he believes others expect of him. If children see themselves as unworthy of respect they are likely to accept abuse as something they deserve. Those that see themselves as unlovable or not capable often lack motivation and accept failure as a reflection of their lack of ability. Children with self-images of "troublemaker" feel more comfortable when they are acting out, challenging authority, being defiant, or getting in trouble than when they are being praised for their good behavior. On the other hand, a child who is referred to as a star and a leader is likely to act in more positive ways.

For example, a well-known Football Hall of Fame quarterback reported that he was speaking in a penitentiary and asked the inmates, "How many of you were told by your parents that someday you would likely end up in jail?" When almost every hand went up, he realized how important it was that his parents had always said to him "Someday you're going to be a star!" What a difference it made in his behavior!

ॐ ॐ ॐ

What is identity and how is it formed?

The sense of identity begins at an early age, even before children begin to walk or talk, as it stems initially from parental feedback. Children develop as psychological mirrors, reflecting the feelings expressed to them verbally, physically, psychologically, and emotionally. They begin to develop feelings of being loved and being OK, or of falling short and being rejected based on the feedback they have taken in. If you are anxious and fearful about your children or their activities, your children are likely to doubt their own abilities. On the other hand, if you are at ease with yourself, your children are more likely to reflect the same confident feelings about themselves.

The feelings you express when your child is undergoing toilet training, starting nursery school or kindergarten, following directions, learning to read, or learning a new skill are likely to determine whether your child feels confident, fearful, or inadequate in later situations. Likewise, the feelings you express regarding your child's accomplishments, creative projects, and efforts determine the degree of pride he or she is likely to feel. Your child will feel good-looking or unattractive, confident or shy, good or bad, depending upon how he or she interprets your reactions and whether you are pleased or convey that the child somehow doesn't quite measure up to your expectations.

The sense of identity is actually composed of multiple self-images. For example, a child might have feelings about himself or herself not only as your son or daughter but also as a sibling, grandchild, friend, team member, as one who can or can't read, or as one who pleases or displeases others. This makes developing a positive self of identity difficult because these images are formed from the feedback received from multiple sources, though as a parent you are likely to have the greatest influence. The feelings your child has about himself may also change as he modifies the significance attached to his different roles. For example, a child may have a positive self-image as a son or daughter. However, there may come a time when being accepted by peers becomes more important and those feelings may not be nearly so positive. It thus becomes important for you to understand what areas are most important to your child, discuss how she feels, what might make her feel better, and what support she would like from you to achieve that.

ಠಠ ಠಠ ಠಠ

It has been mentioned before that a lack of feedback can actually be more damaging to children than negative feedback, for those who receive little or no feedback are unsure about how they are perceived by others. It is important that you, as a parent, provide positive feedback whenever possible to create a positive sense of identity.

Sometimes parents mistakenly cast their children into roles to meet their own personal needs. This can occur when a father pushes his son to be the star football or baseball player he never was, or when a mother dresses her child up to enter beauty contests to satisfy the mother's need for recognition. It can also happen when parents see a child as gifted and expect him or her to always get A's or better grades than other children, or when a son hears that he has to act more responsibly because he is now the man of the family. This might work out well in some situations—but only if the child has the ability to meet those expectations. However, if those expectations are unrealistic, children are apt to suffer from low self-esteem. Setting unrealistic expectations can also put undue stress on children when we reflect stereotypical behavior such as "It's a girl's role to do dishes and take care of younger children," or "We expect you to get all A's this quarter."

ॐ ॐ ॐ

Build a feeling of uniqueness and worth

An important aspect of identity is feeling that one is a unique individual, unlike any other human being on earth. Your child needs to feel capable of being loved and entitled to happiness— that sense of personal worth and self-respect.

Every child needs to understand her uniqueness and realize there is no other child in the world exactly like her. Her fingerprints, DNA, ear formation, and eye print are unique to her. For all children, make the distinction between their behavior and who they really are. This is an effective way to get children to change their behavior. Let them know when their behavior is inconsistent with the beautiful, kind people you believe they really are inside. Help children to get in touch with their inner spirit when they act in ways that reflect that kind nature. Help them believe they are basically good and any other actions may not be truly representative of their true selves. Encourage them to become the significant human beings they were born to become. The Bible states that God loves them, created them uniquely in His image, and will never withhold his love from them.

You may find it necessary on occasion to punish your child's behavior, but try to reaffirm your belief in the positive nature of the child. Research has demonstrated that the easiest way to change a child's negative behavior and low self-concept is to change the way you, the parent, feel about your child. By increasing your respect, interest, and concern for your child, you can change the way your child feels about himself or herself. Behavioral change then comes naturally for both you and your child.

"I don't guess anyone will want to patent my genes."

Another way to build a child's sense of uniqueness is to have him explore a variety of experiences to determine what he enjoys and where his strengths might lie. Such experiences might include learning to play the piano or a musical instrument, learning to ride a bicycle or a horse, playing new games, building models, being exposed to various art experiences, learning new athletic skills, or learning how to be proficient in different academic skills. A word of caution, however! Children can be over-programmed with lessons and activities. Remember, young children learn through play, and all children need time to explore, reflect and dream. Children may make new discoveries and develop passions through simple observations or experiences.

Children need to understand there are multiple ways to learn. Some are more sensitive to visual images than others. Others may learn best by listening or by experiencing concepts through their motor senses. Some seem to have inborn talent in music, others in math, others in art or dance. However, children never know which ways they learn best unless they have multiple experiences learning in different ways. Without such opportunities, they may avoid entering into activities with their peers, believing they have no talent in that area, or they may end up trying out new roles in an unsafe environment.

ఆ◌ ◌)◌ ఆ◌

Children who have a realistic sense of their strengths are more likely to place themselves in situations where they have a good chance of succeeding, and more likely to avoid those situations where they are apt to fail. Such children are not likely to respond defensively to criticism or comments regarding their weaknesses, because they are well aware of them.

Seeing oneself as being unique should not imply that one is better than anyone else—just different. We need to avoid creating children who become conceited because they feel they are better than others. Neither do we wish for them to become so self-centered that they do not value the importance of others. We want our children to sense their uniqueness while at the same time respecting those around them.

ఆ◌ ◌)◌ ఆ◌

Competition can either have a positive or negative impact on how a child feels about himself or herself. Sometimes adults have used children to meet their own needs for recognition. It is easy to slip into the trap of trying to live out our unrealized dreams through the lives of our children. Fathers especially can feel strongly about wanting a child either to participate in competition or to avoid it, as a result of the father's own experience as a child.

Some activities to consider:

1. Help your child discover how he is unique. Take a magnifying glass and have him look carefully at his thumbprint. Then have him use the magnifying glass to look at someone else's thumb, to see how different they are.

2. Have your child lie on a large piece of butcher paper so you can trace an outline of her body. Then have her color it, drawing her face and clothes. Have her put it on her bedroom door.

3. Point out the skills and qualities you observe that make your child unique and special.

4. Talk with your children about how they see themselves and their behavior versus how they would like to be known. What would they change? Who are their heroes? What qualities do they have that are heroic or admirable?

Youth sports are a great opportunity to build self-esteem and personal skills because sports and athletic ability are highly valued in our society. Participating in sports can promote increased self-esteem, because children feel better about themselves as they see themselves develop valued skills that they didn't have before. Sports can also provide a great opportunity for children to learn to work together as a team. Competitive sports provide multiple opportunities for developing mental toughness, but competition can also be a source of great frustration and discouragement.

Most children enjoy competition—if they feel they have an opportunity to win or participate on an equal level. However, when children are pushed into competitive situations where they have no chance of winning or where there is undue pressure placed on them to excel, they are likely to get down on themselves and convince themselves there is something wrong with them. An important key is the child's attitude in entering a competitive situation. When children feel it is vitally important to their parents that they win, they sometimes worry that they are going to lose the love and respect of their parents if they don't succeed. However, when children are given the choice of competing or not, with no parental pressure, the adverse effects of competition are minimized and the child is likely to benefit by learning valuable skills and attitudes.

ତ୍ତ: ତ୍ତ: ତ୍ତ:

Provide unconditional love and positive feedback

All children need to feel a sense of personal worth and unconditional love to have a positive sense of identity and high self-esteem. This unconditional love provides the security of knowing that one is valued, regardless of one's shortcomings or faults. Such unconditional love and feelings of worth normally come from those closest to children, their parents.

Such love must not be conditional on their achievements, but must always be there for them. It is possible for some children to become high achievers and gain recognition from others and yet not feel good about themselves for a variety of reasons. Gifted girls, for example, sometimes downplay their intellectual prowess in order to feel more accepted by their peers. Also, some children believe their parents' love for them is based only on being a high achiever. This was the case with Conrad, a tall, good-looking tenth grade student. He seemed to have everything going for him as an honor student and a student body officer; yet he committed suicide because he received a poor grade in school. His perception was that he had failed to meet his parents' expectations, and that as a result they would never love him again. This is why it is so important to let your child know that your love can always be counted on, that your love is not dependent on a certain level of achievement.

The same is true regarding behavior. You don't have to accept or excuse poor behavior, but you should not withdraw your expressions of love from your children when they misbehave or disappoint. At times, this can be extremely difficult. Your expressions of disappointment in your children's behavior should not relate to your expressions of love.

Unconditional love can be demonstrated in numerous ways—both verbal and nonverbal. Research has documented the importance of physical touching. An affectionate hug or pat on the back is one important way in which to express love and affection. A hug is often worth more to your child than just saying "I love you." But you need to find multiple ways of expressing your affection, even when your child has disappointed you or has found himself in trouble.

ೲ ೲ ೲ

One guideline is to treat your child as if he or she were the child of your best friend. Your child is an important person! When you do this, the rest comes naturally. You automatically react to your child in ways that build a strong sense of identity. Laugh together, share ideas and experiences, and express your love in various little ways.

This means listening to your children and taking their ideas into serious consideration. Avoid yelling at them, making fun of them in front of others, putting down their ideas as silly, or urging them to keep their mouths shut. This can be quite damaging to anyone's sense of worth. Give children an opportunity to express themselves, be included in family discussions, and receive explanations for things they don't understand.

A healthy sense of identity requires children to have a realistic view of themselves, not inflated by flattering comments, but accurate knowledge of their strengths, shortcomings, and how others see them. It must therefore be well grounded in reality. This requires honest feedback. The feedback given should be balanced so children gain an accurate picture of themselves and how they are perceived by others. Unfortunately, in most families children receive more negative criticism than positive feedback.

Positive feedback doesn't mean flattery or false praise. This can result in an inflated ego. Children are well aware when praise is not truly deserved. It leads them to discount your words and not trust your judgment. An important guideline is to praise or give positive attention to actual accomplishments, rather than praising the child himself or herself as being "good." It helps if your praise or positive feedback is in the form of a descriptive phrase of encouragement such as "I really like the way you stick with things even when it is hard for you."

ॐ ॐ ॐ

Children who have difficulty in school or who have particular handicaps or special needs usually require great amounts of positive feedback. They experience far more frustration and criticism or ridicule from their peers than the average child. These children need to be aware that they possess many fine qualities—a happy smile, a good-natured disposition, the ability to be helpful to others, skill at playing games, a strong sense of what is "right." Your child may be completely unaware of the significance of these qualities unless you draw attention to them.

Teach your child to make positive self-statements about himself or herself, for we all talk with ourselves. Psychologists say we engage in self-talk sometimes as much as 40,000 times a day, and 60% of the time it is negative. Encourage your child to use positive self-talk. Here are some examples:

"I can achieve this if I really try hard."

"I know that I can solve this problem if I keep working at it."

"I am a valuable, worthwhile person."

"I may have difficulty reading, but I am sure good in math."

Be careful about the comments you make to your friends and relatives that have negative connotations for your child. Comments such as, "She's my baby," or "John is the slow one in the family," or "Sarah is the non-reader in the family" build or reinforce negative self-images. It is far more valuable to make comments regarding your child's strengths such as, "Brenda works so hard on her schoolwork," or "Paul was a great help to me today."

ॐ ॐ ॐ

Research studies in reading, spelling, and math indicate that drawing attention to children's skills and strengths can result in improved achievement, where criticism results in no increase in achievement.

Some activities to consider:

1. Discuss with your children why a young person might be gifted intellectually and yet not feel good about himself or herself.

2. Have your children share how they believe their grandparents feel about them. Ask them to compare this with how they believe their parents feel about them, or their siblings or friends.

3. Find multiple ways to express love for your child. Use Post-It Notes to place messages on a pillow, inside a lunch box, or on a mirror.

4. Young children can look at vegetables and fruits and talk about how they are alike and different and sort them by color or shape. Ask your young children to compare vegetables to people, to show how each or us is unique and valuable.

Help children capitalize on their strengths

Research has demonstrated that the most successful individuals are those who capitalize on their strengths. Most children find it easier to identify their weaknesses than their strengths. You can help your children by drawing attention to their attributes of character, positive characteristics, skills, and accomplishments rather than focusing on their weak areas.

❧ ❧ ❧

Bob's son was one of those children with learning difficulties. He was diagnosed with dyslexia. Reading and writing were especially difficult for him. To counteract this, Bob always tried to give recognition to his son's spatial and mechanical abilities. His son enjoyed taking apart anything mechanical that ran, including clocks, lawn motor engines, and motorcycles. Unfortunately, he wasn't always successful at putting them back together again correctly. However, he became a successful motorcycle racer and mechanic. As he matured, he realized he had other ambitions so he began to set goals for himself. He decided to complete his education, and worked hard to become a commercial airline pilot, a career he dearly enjoys today. He capitalized on his strengths rather than worry about his weaknesses, and accomplished great things.

❧ ❧ ❧

Sometimes a child is aware of a particular strength, but it is not one that he or she values. For example, Georgia, a beautiful sixth grader with dark brown eyes, was particularly good in math, but she really valued being popular with her peers so tended to discount the significance of her math skill. It was more important to her that she have good friends rather than good grades. It wasn't until later that she began to realize the significance of this math skill and went on to major in mathematics. It is important to identify for your children strengths you believe they have, even if they don't value them at the time.

Consider for a moment what qualities you value most in your child. Here are some qualities you might see in your child that you value:

- ◆ a sense of humor
- ◆ a caring nature they empathy for others
- ◆ honesty
- ◆ persistence
- ◆ a helpful nature
- ◆ a beautiful smile

While such characteristics are critical to success in many occupations, most children do not appreciate these qualities unless their attention is drawn to their significance. So it is important for you as a parent to point out how valuable these qualities are. You might even mention how your child might use these qualities in the work he or she might do as an adult.

One way of highlighting your child's strengths is to refer to her as a budding scientist, potentially a great teacher, an entrepreneur, a potential concert virtuoso, or a mechanic who can fix anything! It is easier for us to pay particular attention to grades on the report card, but some of these other qualities may prove to be far more important than good grades or test scores.

❧ ❧ ❧

From time to time you may hear children make negative comments about themselves. This is a time when they need to be reassured and perhaps view themselves from a more realistic perspective. Point out to your children some of their positive qualities that compensate for the negative ones they see. One first grade child is reported to have said during a class discussion of strengths and weaknesses, "I may not be perfect, but parts of me are excellent." We wish every child could have that same realistic acceptance of self.

Help your child see how he is growing and changing. If there is one aspect of himself that he really dislikes, have him set a goal to change it (if it is something he can change). Reaffirm your belief in his innate goodness, worth and capability. Point out hidden wellsprings of talent or ability he may not see in himself. This contributes to his positive sense of identity.

Some activities to consider:

1. Have children develop a notebook of things that make them feel proud.

2. Post two photos of your child by their bed—one of the child with the family and one of the child being successful at something for the first time. These photos are likely to feature in their dreams at night.

3. Ask your child what she feels are her best qualities or strengths. Share your perceptions as well. Talk about how important you believe those qualities are.

4. Make a medallion for each new skill accomplished. Create an "I Can Do" list.

5. Have your child make a family tree showing the qualities or strengths they admire in each of their family members.

ରେ ଓଡ଼ ରେ

Develop intrapersonal skills

Howard Gardner, the well known Harvard professor, named intra-personal intelligence as one of the eight intelligences. Intra-personal skills are those that enable children to fully understand themselves and their emotions. It is sometimes referred to as "emotional intelligence." One must be able to understand oneself before one is likely to understand others or develop the interpersonal skills required to work cooperatively with others. This is a particularly difficult task for the adolescent. The familiar and comfortable self known from childhood is in a state of dramatic change. Changes in sexual development, size, muscular development, body shape and weight all necessitate modification of one's childhood self-concept. Up to this point, young people have typically learned to act in accord with adult expectations. But now they are anxious to gain peer acceptance. During adolescence, children may develop conflicting emotions about their appearance and abilities. You can help with this by discussing with them the emotions they have and how they might deal with those feelings.

ଚତ୍ ଚଠ୍ ଚତ୍

An important intrapersonal skill is the ability to deal with emotions in socially acceptable ways. Many children have a fear of expressing true emotions such as fear, anxiety, loss, or shame. It is important for you to establish an environment that confirms your children's right to express emotions, and for you to teach them the vocabulary to express the feelings they have. This is especially helpful for young children. As children grow older they will need to develop the practice of choosing how they want to deal with their feelings, rather than responding without thinking.

You can help develop the skill of dealing with emotions by teaching children words that can be used to express feelings—words such as *frustrated, discouraged, disappointed, jealous, anxious, delighted,* and *ecstatic.* When children become aware of the feelings they have, they can use these words to communicate the nature of their feelings. Specific words that convey nuances of feeling are so much better for communicating than just feeling "mad" or "glad."

From time to time, children are likely to experience someone saying mean things about them, or someone putting them down. When this happens, children need to realize that there are a variety of options for dealing with the intense feelings this causes. You can help by exploring with your children the variety of options they have for responding, so they don't just respond automatically without thinking. This is difficult for most children. But it is a skill that can be learned. We will explore some of the options for dealing with peers in the next chapter.

Delayed gratification is another skill that helps your child develop emotional wellness. Research indicates that those children who never learn to delay their impulse for gratification experience continued difficulties all through their lifetime. For young children, it can be a simple statement like, "I can help you with that as soon as I finish what I am doing," or "You need to wait to get that until you save your allowance." The ability to delay gratification fosters patience and thinking ahead instead of demanding, "I want it now!"

Some activities to consider:

1. Talk with your children about the automatic response system that comes up for them when they feel hurt, rage, upset, or revengeful. Help them develop effective ways of dealing with their emotions before they respond to others.

2. When children are filled with anger or frustration, have them picture filling a hot-air balloon with all those hostile feelings. Have them picture taking this balloon to a large field and letting it go so their troubles drift away with the breeze.

3. Discuss with your children situations that are most likely to upset them and bring them to the point of losing control. Help them find some ways of dealing with this flood of emotions.

4. To help your young children communicate feelings, have them draw faces and label them with feelings they are experiencing.

Spend quality time with your child

So much of our communication with children is in the nature of directions, admonishments, and reminders. Because we want the best for our children, it is always a temptation to instruct, advise, or correct. This is why it is important to take time to give your child undivided attention, time with you without interruption. This we call "quality time." Children realize that parents have lots to do, so when you take time to give them undivided attention it reinforces their significance and sense of worth. This should be a time when you listen and your child can talk about things that are important to him or her.

Communicating with your child needs to be ongoing. It should not fall into a question-and-answer session. Begin by talking about the commonplace. Sooner or later, real concerns will be voiced, usually when you are not making eye contact. This is especially true for boys, who are more likely to talk when working with you on a project, when you are preparing dinner and they are in the same room, or at bedtime when the lights are out and you are saying goodnight. Another good time is while you are driving and chatting. One mother said she deliberately gets lost when children begin to talk about matters of importance so she can prolong the drive and the discussion.

꒰ ꒱ ꒰

The key here is the importance of listening for feelings or real meaning and then trying to check to make certain that you understand what your child is trying to say. A major concern children have is being misunderstood. Most adolescents believe their parents don't understand them. Normally, when a child feels that mother or father truly understands what he is trying to convey, the situation becomes much calmer and more rational. Understanding your child and helping her communicate accurately depends on your ability to recognize, interpret, and acknowledge her personal feelings. This enables you to help your child better manage difficult situations. Your listening will be most effective when you try to remember these points:

- ◆ Listen without making judgments as to what is right or wrong.
- ◆ Avoid telling your child what he or she should do.
- ◆ Accept how your child feels rather than telling him/her how he or she should feel.
- ◆ Validate your child's feelings by using statements such as "You seem to be really frustrated," or "It sounds like you feel no one cares" to let the child know that you understand the feelings expressed.

For single parents or working parents, who cannot spend a great deal of time with their children or who might not be at home when their child returns from school, a tape recorder may be a solution. The tape recorder can be placed on the kitchen counter to have your child share the day's events before those events are forgotten. This can be a great way to communicate and is almost as good as being there. These taped messages can be one way to share the joys and problems of the day when your schedule prevents you from doing that. Being able to communicate by cell phone is another effective solution.

༄ ༄ ༄

When you ask your child what happened at school, the typical response is apt to be "nothing." A teacher friend sent a newsletter home with the title, "Much Ado About Nothing" to share all the things that had been going on in the classroom. One single parent we know directs the dinnertime conversation by asking, "What's the best thing that happened to you today and what's the worst thing that happened to you today." Everybody shares.

Hang out with each of your children if you have more than one child and do things one-on-one, without the child having to compete with other siblings to get your attention. Schedule your activity with each child at a regular time so that your children know that if you don't have time for them at the particular moment they wish to talk, they will have that chance when their time comes up.

Some activities to consider:

1. Have your children share how they would most like to spend time with you if you were to set aside a special time just for them.

2. Ask your children about the ways in which you attempt to communicate your unconditional love for them, what things they appreciate most, and what is most meaningful to them.

3. Help your children reach their inner self and the perfect, kind, considerate human being that resides there.

4. Take your young child for a walk. Listening walks are great ways to become calm and reflective. Young children can hear so many sounds around them as they walk without talking.

Summary

Developing a healthy, realistic sense of identity is the key to positive mental health. The child who has self-knowledge, who recognizes his strengths and weaknesses, who has a strong sense of personal worth and who has strong intrapersonal skills is likely to be happy and well adjusted. To achieve this, parents need to provide unconditional love, positive feedback, quality personal attention, and guidance in self-understanding. Most of all, you need to honor the uniqueness of your child and demonstrate caring for who he is and not what he can achieve.

Chapter 5
Key#3: Fostering a Sense of Belonging

"When you have a true interaction with others,
huge new regions of yourself bubble up from within."
Brian Swimmer

꒒ ꒒ ꒒

The sense of belonging or connectedness has long been thought to be a basic human need. It stems from feeling that one is an accepted member of something larger than oneself. Children need a strong sense of belonging in order for them to want to share, take turns, contribute to the welfare of others, accept others, or have a sense of social justice.

Significance of belonging

We naturally seek the acceptance or approval of friends or others and desire to feel that we belong to a group that accepts us. This need is evident as early as age five or six, and becomes increasingly important as children reach adolescence.

It's easy to see, in the behavior of children and adults, the characteristics of those who lack this sense of belonging or social acceptance. Lack of belonging is typically expressed in behaviors like avoiding social contacts or being excessively assertive or aggressive. Some children are naturally shy, but often shyness comes about as a result of insecurity when young people are with others who are not their close friends. Sometimes, feeling a lack of social acceptance is expressed through behaviors such as boasting, bragging, or bullying. Some children express their feelings of non-acceptance by alienating others before the others have a chance to hurt or reject them. They find it easier to be rejected if they behave in ways that they know others won't like, so they can then rationalize why they don't have any friends.

When children reach the age of adolescence, 90% of their motivation seems to stem from the desire to feel important in the eyes of their peers. Many resort to extreme ways of achieving this. George, a curly-haired redhead who was short for his age, sought to gain group approval by clowning around in class, constantly showing off. Cynthia also felt the need for social acceptance, but she tried to gain this by trying to be grown up. She smoked in front of her peers, wore sexy clothes and used makeup to attract the attention of the boys. Both were trying to compensate for a lack of belonging or social acceptance.

ଚଚ **ଚଚ** ଚଚ

For adolescent girls, research indicates that being popular and attractive to boys are the two most important factors in their lives. They spend hours grooming and selecting clothes to appear more attractive. For boys, being popular with the girls and being recognized for athletic prowess among their male peers stands out as significant determiners of their self-esteem. Boys between the ages of 12 and 16 take pride in developing their muscles, and enjoy testing their strength and skill against others. The need to belong has also been determined to be a prime reason for adolescents joining gangs. Belonging to a gang can give youth with low self-esteem a feeling of power, support and belonging which they have not gained through individual means.

As a parent, you can reduce this need for peer recognition by developing strong feelings of acceptance and belonging in the family, and by helping your child develop effective social skills. Those children who feel accepted at home and comfortable with others are not likely to feel driven by the need to gain peer acceptance.

Role of the family

You can establish the foundation for the sense of belonging at home by making certain that everyone in the family is treated with respect. Value your children's ideas and input. Preserve their right to privacy and make a conscious effort to have them believe they are valuable members of the family. Your children need to believe that they are contributing to the family and that others in the family contribute to their welfare. This is their first experience at being a member of a social group.

This sense of being an important part of the family can be achieved by planning family activities together. Playing and working together as a family unit builds the closeness that children need. Here are examples of activities the family can do together:

- ◆ Plan family picnics.
- ◆ Take vacations together.
- ◆ Go on camping outings together.
- ◆ Attend sports or musical events.
- ◆ Play games together.
- ◆ Read to one another.
- ◆ Discuss and work on family problems.
- ◆ Sing together.
- ◆ Help each other with schoolwork or tasks around the home.
- ◆ Work together on joint family projects.

Give your children opportunities to have experiences with members of their extended family—grandparents, aunts and uncles, cousins, and other relatives. This helps them relate to an extended family and contributes to their feeling of belonging. It also enables them to become familiar with their family history. When children can feel proud of their family and cultural heritage, it builds that sense of belonging and identity. Share with your children your family's history and how they got to where they are. Activities you can pursue include tracing your family heritage by creating a family tree; sharing family pictures of yourself as a child and as an adolescent; and telling family stories. Children enjoy hearing stories about their parents and grandparents when they were young, especially if the stories are about misadventures or misbehaviors!

Share with your children what you know about your family's culture and the traditions of that culture. Have a special night to celebrate that culture by listening to music, seeing a movie, having special food, or talking with relatives or friends from that culture. Most families are a combination of several cultures so it may be that you will want to celebrate a different family culture each month. The object is to make children feel connected and proud of their family's culture, whether it is Irish, Hispanic, Italian, German, Vietnamese, or Nigerian.

Having meals together can be another way to strengthen family bonds. Unfortunately, this is difficult for most families because of working schedules and commitment to youth activities like Little League, soccer league, church groups, and so on. However, children who grow up in families that eat together have stronger feelings of belonging than those who do not. Eating together can provide a great opportunity to teach effective listening skills, as children listen while members of the family share experiences and issues of concern. It can be an opportunity to give special attention to each member of the family by having a family meal where the spotlight is on one child. Give each member of the family a chance to say something nice about the person in the spotlight—something that the child did that was appreciated, or something positive about them.

Create your own family traditions that have meaning for your children. Family traditions regarding birthdays and special holidays sometimes mean more to children than we realize. They often want the same birthday cake every year or go to the same place repeatedly for family vacations. Bob and his wife, Nancy, typically rented a house for Thanksgiving where the family could all be together for the holiday. One Thanksgiving Bob and Nancy were traveling and could not be with their children, who were now older and on their own for this holiday. The tradition was important enough to the children that they, themselves, chipped in and rented a house so they could maintain the tradition.

Marilyn also remembers the importance of Thanksgiving memories. One year she was so busy being a principal of an elementary school that she thought she would skip making pies and some other parts of the family dinner and buy them instead. That is, until she talked with her granddaughter, Sarah, who was about four at the time. "Grandma, Grandma, I'm so excited! We can find all the pretty leaves again and decorate the table and I can help you roll out the dough when we make pies!" Marilyn realized she had been making more than pies. She had been making traditions and memories. She later started a memory basket and filled it with items such as seashells from an outing at the beach, or a special stone from a special walk, or even a button from a favorite dress. Her grandchildren still contribute to the "Memory Basket."

By engaging in such family activities, your child will gain many of the social skills necessary to feel comfortable in other social situations and gain the acceptance of others.

"Larry says it's his 'extended' family."

Some activities to consider:

1. As a family, plan special traditions you might establish for your family to celebrate holidays. Such traditions might include decorating the Christmas tree together while having hot cider and cookies, making a card for each member of the family for Valentine's Day, etc.

2. Honor your family's heritage by having special nights to celebrate your family's heritage and culture. Talk about where your family came from. Show pictures. Point out on a map the location of your ancestors. Prepare traditional food, play music, or watch a video to share that culture with your children.

3. Do fun things as a family—go bowling, biking, hiking, boating, camping, or play games together. Plan special events to do as a family: go to the zoo, spend a day at a lake, go bowling, attend a sporting event, go on a family hike, go camping.

4. Talk with your child about everyday things that interest him or her. Make time to play with your child each day.

5. Let your child choose a birthday menu—whether it's pizza or birthday pie.

Relationships and interaction among siblings can also have an impact on how children feel about themselves. Parents are inclined to treat older children differently from younger children. They may give the older children more attention, and may expect more from them. The first-born child usually benefits from being the oldest, possibly the biggest, and the first to reach many milestones. Studies indicate that first-born children benefit from the attention they receive, not only from their parents but also from their younger siblings. Thus it is not surprising that as children they usually have higher self-esteem and perhaps tend to be more competitive than their younger siblings. This has been found to be true for both boys and girls. Here are some interesting statistics about first-born children:

- ◆ Of the first twenty-three astronauts sent into outer space, twenty-one were first-borns.
- ◆ All seven astronauts in the original Mercury program were first-borns.
- ◆ More than half the United States presidents were first-borns.
- ◆ First-borns are over-represented among *Who's Who in America* and *American Men and Women of Science,* as well as among Rhodes scholars and professors.

The most reasonable explanation for this is not that being first-born has any genetic benefit. Rather, parents tend to have higher expectations of their first-born children. In addition, these children tend to get a lot of adult attention. These two factors alone make a significant difference in how children turn out.

◌◦ ◌◦ ◌◦

When there are just two children in the family, the birth of the second child means that the attention previously showered on the first-born is suddenly directed towards the younger child. The older sibling might feel resentment and jealousy: though these feelings can usually be overcome by the older child taking on the role of older brother or sister helping to care for the baby. This situation may lead to the younger child receiving a great deal of attention, being treated as a "baby" or being spoiled by not being given responsibilities. As a result, the younger child's self-esteem is rarely as high as that of the older child.

The most unfortunate child is usually the "middle child" of three or more children. A middle child may be unable to do the things that the oldest child does, and generally receives less attention than the "baby" in the family. As a result, many middle children suffer from low self-esteem, seeking ways to compensate for this throughout much of their lives.

What does this mean for you as a parent? You know that siblings and birth order can impact a child's attitudes and development; knowing this, you can make a conscious effort to compensate for any adverse effects you observe in all of your children.

ॐ ॐ ॐ

Dealing with sibling rivalry

Sibling rivalry often arises when children believe they must compete for your attention, or when they resent attention gained by a sibling. As a parent, you must let each child know he is special to you in a different way. Make certain each child also has equal time for your personal attention. When the family engages in activities like playing games together, taking trips together, and working together, family bonds are strengthened and sibling rivalry reduced.

One of the characteristics of effective families is having a peaceful atmosphere in the home that reduces rivalry or resentment. Encourage children to support their siblings and family members rather than teasing or picking on them. The simple statement "We are a family. We love each other and support each other because that's what families are all about!" establishes a value and a standard that reduces sibling conflicts. (It also helps when you convince siblings they need to attend a piano recital or a performance of one of their brothers or sisters!)

ॐ ॐ ॐ

It seems to be natural for children to get on each others nerves from time to time, and even to fight with each other. When your children engage in conflicts with each other, you can't always determine blame or dictate solutions for them, but you can teach them ways of dealing with such situations. You need to teach your children how you want them to resolve the family conflicts that arise, instead of encouraging them to just tattle on each other and have you solve the conflict. Encourage your children to adopt the point of view that conflicts don't have to end up with a winner and a loser, but instead should be resolved in ways that satisfy both parties and avoid further escalation. Help siblings to see each conflict as a challenge for them to find a solution themselves. If they are unable to resolve a particular issue peacefully, a family meeting might be in order to find ways of addressing the problem.

To reduce conflict rivalry among siblings it is important for each child to feel he or she has a special place in your heart. This can be emphasized when a special time is set aside at least once a week for individual attention without interruption from the other siblings. This might enable you to play a special game with one who likes to play games and a time playing outside with another sibling who prefers an outdoor activity. Each needs to feel he or she is unique and respected as a unique individual, important in your eyes.

Some activities to consider:

1. When siblings are angry with each other, have them take turns fully expressing how they feel and why. Be sure each child expresses himself without making accusations, while the other sibling listens.

2. Have each member of the family, especially brothers and sisters, identify the kind of support they would like from others in the family. Get a commitment from each to provide that support.

3. Have young children play a game that involves taking turns, or let them work together on a project like making cookies or putting on a play.

Understanding the paradox of being a unique individual and a member of a group

You must help your child understand the problems of being a unique individual and at the same time just one member of a group. For example, when your child is in school, he can't act as an individual and always do what he wants to do when he wants to do it. As a group member the child has to learn to follow group rules and consider others in the group. He needs to learn how to take turns and help others.

ക‍  ‍ക

Understanding the struggle for balance between being a unique individual and participating as a member of a group is difficult for some children. Oftentimes there can be a conflict between individual needs and the needs and rights of others. There are times when children must forego their own needs for the greater collective need of the group. Knowing how to deal with this is a critical social skill that really helps children in school. Teach your child to recognize that she is a unique individual, but that there will be times when she is also a valuable member of the family. Being a part of a group requires a different set of skills and behaviors than being an individual. In every social situation, there exists a code of expected behavior. Helping your children to understand this enables them to realize that if they choose not to follow the established rules or code of behavior they are apt to get in trouble or be shunned or rejected by others. However, children should be encouraged to adhere to their own code of ethics and not join in when their peers choose to engage in risky or forbidden behavior. There are probably going to be times when their peers decide to engage in drinking liquor, smoke, or destroy property. Learning to stick to one's values and not engage in the behavior of the group is a valuable social skill for children to develop.

ക‍ ‍ക

Develop interpersonal skills

Developing interpersonal skills will help your children function more effectively in social and group situations, as well as strengthening their feelings of belonging. Learning how to listen carefully to others is a critical social skill. It takes some children years to learn to take turns when talking, listen carefully to what is being said by others, and contribute to the discussion without dominating it. This skill, when developed at home, can make a significant contribution to a child's adjustment at school. Children also need to learn to listen without making judgments of others. This is especially important in helping to understand and relate to those from different cultures or family backgrounds. It is dangerously easy for children to judge others without fully listening or understanding who they are.

∞ ∞ ∞

Empathy and learning how to be of assistance to others requires the ability to look at situations from the perspective of another. People who understand the feelings of others are better able to work in cooperative situations. Each person brings to any given situation her own perception and feelings. Being able to share one's perceptions and feelings and to interpret those perceptions and feelings of others is a valuable skill for children to learn. Learning to give clear "I" messages and feedback can aid in communicating with others. Stating "I hear you saying...", as a means of making certain one has correctly interpreted what one has heard, lets the other person know he has been heard, and provides him with the opportunity to further clarify if needed. An easy way to teach this is to stop and ask from time to time, when you are reading a story with your child, just how your child believes the person in the story might be feeling, or have your child offer an acceptable solution or alternative to a problem in the story. You can also help your child develop the skill of anticipating what might be needed in the situation and how the child could help if she was in that situation. Literature is invaluable in helping children look at things from multiple points of view.

ॐ ॐ ॐ

Another valuable social skill which children can learn from the family is how to contribute to the welfare of others. From family interaction, children can be taught how to show respect and concern for others, and how they might be helpful in a given situation. You must be careful how you model this, however! Don't be like the father who was observed grabbing a bag of candy from his daughter, who was evidently reluctant to share the candy with her sister. As he snatched the bag away from her, he shouted, "Now share, damn it!" This probably didn't do much to encourage the sharing he was trying to develop. Most likely it caused resentment, anger, helplessness, or disrespect rather than fostering positive feelings for sharing. In such situations, it is important that you try to remain patient, showing the respect and caring you want your children to display.

Some activities to consider:

1. Play listening games with children with a telephone and have them repeat what they heard.

2. Brainstorm a list of questions that could be used in talking with someone else that would give your children insights to help them understand and know that other person better.

3. Discuss with children the topic of body language and how body language reflects how others are feeling. Have them demonstrate how they use body language to express their feelings.

4. Help your child learn how to offer hospitality to others. When a friend of theirs comes over, your child can make him or her more comfortable by offering a snack or letting the guest play with a favorite toy.

Interpersonal skills can be further developed by having children participate in team sports, youth organizations, church activities or neighborhood groups. Participation in such activities provides opportunities to apply group skills and further learn how to be a contributing member of a team or group.

Effective use of family meetings

Meeting with all members of the family to plan activities, discuss problems and address personal concerns can be an effective way to solve family problems and reduce conflicts. Such meetings require total family involvement and complete respect for what individuals share. It's important to make certain that each member is given full attention and respect as he or she shares personal concerns. Some families use a salt shaker or an object like a teddy bear to pass from one to another to make certain that only the one with the object talks while others listen. Family meetings can strengthen closeness, cooperation, and belonging.

ॐ ॐ ॐ

Family meetings can be informal, or they can be structured in a more formal way with a set time each week and an agenda developed with the items individuals wish to discuss. Decisions made in family meetings should be made by consensus rather than by majority vote. This makes it more likely that everyone can live with the decision made. Planning a family outing or activity to do together should be on the agenda of each family meeting. Family meetings are also good times to compliment family members and thank them for their contributions to the family.

Young children will probably encounter people outside the family who act aggressively or who hurt their feelings. The children need to learn how to solve these problems without your intervention. While we really don't want children to fight, it is not healthy to set rules that result in their bottling up their feelings. Children who are brought up never to fight can end up as passive victims of every bully they meet in school. Hence, rather than directing them "Don't ever fight!" help them develop a set of strategies to use, so fighting is only a last resort.

An important lesson for children to learn is to stop and remember there are a variety of ways of dealing with any situation. This might mean allowing oneself a "cooling off period" before doing anything. It might require walking away and not dealing with a situation while the child is flooded with emotion. Another option might be for the child to confront the individual who hurt him with an honest statement of how he feels, allowing the other person to share his or her position, and then trying to find an acceptable way of resolving the conflict. The child may find out that his hurt was caused accidentally. If, on the other hand, the child did something to cause the problem, he needs to learn how to apologize effectively.

ॐ ॐ ॐ

Teach your children the value of compromising and how to negotiate agreements so that both parties feel satisfied. This can be a valuable leadership skill and more effective than demanding or imposing one's position on others. Finally, children may need to decide whether to take the matter into their own hands with all of the consequences, or whether it would be best to seek someone else to mediate the situation.

As children reach the age of adolescence, they will probably experience situations where their classmates or friends prey on their need for acceptance by creating tightly knit groups of friends who cultivate an air of privilege and exclusivity. People in such cliques make themselves feel good by making those outside the circle feel ostracized and unworthy. Those left out are often kids who may feel socially awkward and who may have an underdeveloped sense of confidence and self-esteem. Girls are frequently victims of catty behavior and nasty comments, judging each other on appearance and material possessions. Boys' cliques behave similarly, but emphasis is more on athletic ability, physical prowess, and appearance. Because of children's need for acceptance and belonging, these groups can seem all-important in your child's life.

To help your child through such situations, it is best not to interject yourself into the situation. Don't approach your child's peers or their parents. Instead, it is important to listen to your child and encourage him or her to talk about the social situation. Be available to talk and offer support, but allow your child to come up with her own solution. Talk with her about what is right and just. It may help for your child to engage in different activities, new interests, or a new group of friends. It can be a valuable learning experience, teaching the child how not to treat others as well as how to gain new friends.

Most teenagers experience being teased or picked on by an older student who acts like a bully. There are times when bullies need to be confronted. Bob's grandson, Frank, a freshman in high school, was being tormented by an upper classman who seemed to delight in hitting Frank on the back of the head whenever he passed him in the hall. Finally, Frank had had enough, so he developed a strategy for dealing with this bully. The next time he was hit, Frank suddenly turned around and faced his tormentor, walked right up to him and said, "I've had enough of that." As his tormentor began to back away, Frank stepped forward so that he was right in his tormentor's face. Frank stated, "I won't take that anymore so just lay off!" His tormentor was so startled, he never bothered him again. Bullies enjoy picking on others and seeing them cry or be miserable. When they meet up against someone willing to stand up for himself it spoils the fun, so the bully is likely to find someone else to pick on.

ॐ ॐ ॐ

If your child continues being picked on by a bully or physically threatened and safety becomes a concern, it is well to talk with your child's teacher or principal to make certain that the situation doesn't escalate and your child is not physically harmed.

When children learn to stop and consider various options before acting, they are exercising self-control, a valuable social skill. Guide your child to think through situations and come up with strategies the child believes will accomplish his or her objectives. The most effective way of teaching such skills is for you as a parent to model moderation and temperance in dealing with your own emotions and resist the temptation to step in and solve children's problems. By allowing children the freedom to handle their own problems, you not only strengthen their skills but also build their feelings of self-confidence.

Some activities to consider:

1. Encourage your children to practice random acts of kindness by thinking of something they could do for others. Ask at the dinner table from time to time what act of kindness each child performed today, and encourage this as a daily practice.

2. Help your children brainstorm responses they could make to handle "put-downs" they might receive from classmates. Such responses might be using humor or commenting, "That's because you don't really know me," or "Thanks for sharing your opinion."

3. Have your children talk about some of the conflict situations they could find themselves in within the next year, what they might say, and how they could deal with these situations.

4. Help your child express his/her feelings and help them brainstorm what they might say to one of their peers in different situations.

Dealing with peer pressures

As children reach adolescence, a number of changes occur. Along with physical change, it's an age of insecurity, mood shifts, temper tantrums, defiance, self-consciousness, and peer pressures. It is natural for young people to want to be with their peers and to be like them. As your child reaches adolescence he or she is apt to experience situations where there will be pressures to conform to the group. Peer pressures can be a danger when children begin to associate with others who use different standards or values. Before such occasions arise you need to encourage your child when faced with such a situation to act as a unique individual, conforming to his or her own standards of ethics and behavior rather than going along with the rest of the group.

∞ ⟨)⟨⟩ ∞

This is a time to reinforce family rules or standards of behavior that all members of the family follow. Talk about the values your family considers important, so that when your children are with their peers they have a set of standards to guide their own behavior. This will help them evaluate themselves and their behavior on the basis of these standards and values. It also helps keep the lines of communication with you open.

Such reinforcing of family values would be important if, for example, your children find themselves being encouraged to smoke, drink, or engage in activities that are not in their own best interests and are contrary to those family values you have set. This is also a time when your child needs to have refusal skills. Being able to say, "No, I don't wish to participate in that," requires role playing at home and being taught how to say "No" in an effective manner. Sometimes it is helpful for children to use the parental "no" to avoid doing things they know are wrong. "Sorry, my parents won't let me" gets them off the hook until they are strong enough to say, "I don't want to do that."

Friends of your children need to be included in your greater circle of family, especially in adolescence. Show your children's friends what it's like to be part of your family. Make an effort to get to know these friends your children have selected, especially the ones who might be a negative influence on your child. It's hard for children with any conscience to persuade your child to engage in immoral or risky behaviors when they have to face and be treated as good friends of the family!

When parents have worked to develop a strong sense of belonging at home, children don't need to compensate for the lack of feelings of belonging by engaging in extreme behavior to gain peer recognition. Children who come from families where they are loved, supported, and are included as contributing members of the family find it easier to become members of other social groups and resist peer pressures.

It is natural to be concerned for your children's welfare, and for you to want some control over their activities. However, your children want to be trusted. It is recommended that you negotiate with them, finding ways in which you can monitor where they are and what they might be doing without their feeling controlled. Take time to check whether there is proper adult supervision at homes where your children will be staying or attending a party. Keep in contact by cell phone at designated times if you feel the need to. Your children may feel embarrassed by calls and often resent them; however, when they know it is because of your love and concern for their welfare, they can understand and better accept it.

Some activities to consider:

1. Talk with your children about the characteristics they consider most important in their friends. Have your children evaluate the degree to which they model those characteristics.

2. Talk with your children about the groups to which family members belong and the behaviors expected of group members in those situations.

3. Have your children describe some situations where their values are likely to be different from those of their peers, and perhaps even challenged by their peers. Discuss what your children might do or say to deal with those situations.

Help your child develop a support group

Having friends, mentors, or other adults to call on for support and guidance can be a great asset to your child. Having an adult mentor has proven to be a major factor in deterring deviant behavior, including crime and violence. A mentor can be a great benefit for your child. Explore with your child whether there is someone she really looks up to, whom she might go to for independent perceptions, advice, or assistance.

In addition to other adults, encourage your child to develop close friends who share interests, values, and judgment. As a parent you can encourage your children to associate with other young people you feel would be a positive influence on them. Invite other young people into your home so they get to know you and your values. Include your children's close friends occasionally as part of the family circle so they also become a source of support for your children, and so they understand your standards and values. Play games with them or encourage your children to invite friends along when you go to the movies or on an outing.

ॐ ॐ ॐ

Encourage service to others

Children need to experience the satisfaction of doing things for others and making a contribution to the welfare of others. When they put in time and effort on good causes, they will feel better about themselves and increase feelings of self-worth. Help your children develop empathy by teaching them to be sensitive to the needs of others. You can do this by talking with them about the characters of a story or TV program and how these characters might be feeling. Encourage your children to act courageously when they are with their friends, to enact justice on behalf of others. Build a sense of justice by discouraging them from picking on others, bullying others, or discriminating against others.

An effective way to build feelings of self-worth is to create opportunities where children can feel valued by others. Build your family into a support group for one another. Do chores together, take on family projects as a group, and ask or share from time to time what kind of support is needed from other family members to achieve goals or make changes in habits. Children gain feelings of importance when they feel that they are contributing to others, so it is important for them to have family chores and learn how to help others.

₰ ₰ ₰

Preschool children can gain these feelings by contributing to chores at home. As they grow older, they can contribute in increasingly significant ways. Feelings of personal worth can also come about through service to others outside the family, such as helping grandparents, neighbors, senior citizens, or people less fortunate. Involve your children when you do something for shut-ins or engage in service to others. Through such activities you are setting a model for them as well as enabling them to feel that they are being of service, too. Your children's contribution to the welfare of others gives them a feeling of being appreciated, builds feelings of personal worth, and creates a feeling of social acceptance and belonging. Working together on a community project can support your role as mentor and model and strengthen family bonds.

By engaging in service activities children learn the value of giving while gaining social skills. The feelings they gain are more significant than activities that merely provide pleasure, such as playing a game, watching cartoons, or playing with friends because they contribute to feelings of personal worth.

Those individuals who most often feel a sense of inner satisfaction in work are those who aim to meet the needs of others, rather than just their own needs. When individuals contribute to the welfare of others, they bond, grow, and develop skills vital to so many professions. These individuals tend to focus their emphasis on those activities that will improve the quality of life for others. Feeling needed by others and making a contribution to their welfare is a primary motivational force for teachers, doctors, nurses, police, and clergy. Whether your child enters such a profession or not, he or she needs to experience the joy of being of service. Encourage your child to shift the emphasis to those activities that will improve the quality of life for others.

If you do everything for your children, they are likely to perceive themselves as inadequate and insignificant, and they will seldom feel satisfied with their situation. It's only when their focus is outside themselves and on the welfare of others that children gain the sense of dignity and self-respect, characteristics of productive well-being. It can also allow a child to escape negative feelings towards himself—by diverting his energy outward, his "troubles" can disappear.

Summary

Children will go to great lengths to feel important in the eyes of others and gain acceptance. However, developing strong feelings of belonging within the family reduces the need for children to engage in extreme behavior to gain that acceptance from peers. Thus, it is important for the family to engage in activities together. Knowing family values, having family discussions and joint decision making all contribute to helping children manage peer conflicts and peer pressure. Experiencing the value of being of service to others adds to feelings of worth and belonging.

☙ ☙☙ ☙

Chapter 6
Key #4: Inspiring a Sense
of Purpose

*"Goals give purpose; purpose gives faith; faith gives courage;
courage gives enthusiasm; enthusiasm gives energy, and energy gives
life. Life is what lifts you over the hurdles and the bar."*

Bob Richards

ༀ ༀ ༀ

Just as "parenting with purpose" requires you to clarify the desired outcomes for your parenting, it's important that your children determine their own purposes in life. Children need to feel that their lives have significance, that the things they do have relevance for what they want to achieve or become. Character traits such as motivation, conviction, determination, perseverance, integrity, and ethical values can all be developed through a sense of purpose.

Most of us would like our children to be motivated by their curiosity, their desire to learn and achieve. We would like for them to strive for higher human needs and values, and to decide what pattern of growth they wish to pursue for themselves. We might hope that our children acquire a strong sense of right and wrong based on fundamental values, so they can live and act with integrity. Most parents would also like their children to enjoy inner satisfaction and achieve a meaningful and fulfilling life, rather than measuring their worth against anyone else.

To be motivated by a sense of purpose, children need to have a sense of security, a positive self-concept or identity, and feel a sense of belonging. Then their internal source of motivation comes naturally, allowing them to focus on the task at hand rather than being concerned about the impression they are making upon others. Children who feel insecure, rejected by others, or who have poor self-concepts are primarily motivated to compensate for those negative feelings, focusing on gaining recognition from others.

Unfortunately, society encourages young people to compare themselves with others—to be better athletically, be more attractive, to have more money or the latest technology. Individuals who focus on being better than others are likely to develop feelings of conceit or a distorted sense of self-worth. Research has also documented that such individuals are more likely to suffer from stress, drug and alcohol use, or disordered eating. In order to achieve self-esteem, it is important that people assume responsibility for their lives, seek positive relationships and work on self-improvement. They need to identify where they would like to improve or a skill they would like to develop, and then focus on how to achieve that objective.

ॐ ॐ ॐ

As young people reach adolescence, many of them lack this sense of purpose. This is often expressed through comments like "I'm bored" or "school is such a drag." When students lack a sense of where they are headed or what is important, it becomes difficult for them to be motivated or to put forth much real effort. They are easily distracted and their energy is wasted much of the time. When parents and teachers urge them to work harder, they resent it and rebel. Many of these students soon give up trying to succeed, thinking that it takes too much effort. The strange thing is that even when they succeed, they are likely to believe their success was because the teacher liked them or perhaps they were just lucky, rather than believing it to be a result of their effort or ability. As a result, they rarely capitalize on that motivating force of inner satisfaction.

It is natural, therefore, that those who lack this sense of purpose are most likely to engage in deviant behaviors such as drug or alcohol abuse, teenage pregnancy, crime and violence, or dropping out of school. Those who attempt suicide typically feel that life itself has no meaning or purpose. On the other hand, when young people have clear visions of what they want to become or what they want to do with their lives, they are less inclined to become involved in such deviant behaviors.

This was made clear when the police came to the school district where Bob served as superintendent to investigate why so few students in the district engaged in drug abuse when drugs were so readily available in the area. After interviewing a number of students, the police found many who responded with statements like "I know where I can get drugs, but I have more important things to do with my life than get involved in drugs." These students, who turned their backs on an early drug culture, seemed to have developed a personal vision of their future that didn't make it worth engaging in such behavior. They understood that any short-term "boost" from drug use would inevitably destroy any chance of achieving their dreams.

ॐ ॐ ॐ

When children have this sense of purpose, they think consciously of what they are trying to do, why they are doing it, and how that fits into their long-range goals. Their energy is clearly focused. They approach tasks with a sense of intention, so are more likely to achieve success. This enables them to set goals for themselves and accomplish what they set out to do. As a result they achieve satisfaction and joy through their work, and look toward the future with a positive outlook. Their motivation might be to have fun or it may be to explore, to build, to understand, to become knowledgeable, or to contribute. However, their source of motivation is internalized rather than being motivated by external factors and what other people think of them.

Some children almost seem to be born with purpose in their lives. From day one, they know what they want to do and set out to do it. We have all read about the child who always wanted to be a doctor or a musician, and who concentrated energy, time, and learning on that goal. However, you, as a parent, can develop this same focus by training your children to be conscious of their intention or purpose whenever they are engaged in an activity.

Some activities to consider:

1. Before your young child starts an activity ask her what her intention is in that activity, or what she hopes to learn from it. Then when she has finished, have her reflect on whether she achieved her purpose.

2. Create stories yourself where your child turns out to be the hero or heroine. Have him tell stories of his own where he is the center of the story.

3. Have your child talk about the vision she has for herself in terms of the characteristics she would like to have, how she would like to be viewed by others, and the contribution she would like to make to the world.

ख़ ख़ख़ ख़

According to reliable research, high expectations for young people are important in building a sense of purpose which results in school achievement. Studies have shown that one of the reasons children lack motivation and underachieve is because no clear expectations have been set for them. When you have high expectations for your children, they will typically try to meet those expectations as long as those expectations are realistic. Set expectations that are appropriate to the age level and ability of the child and what you believe he or she can actually achieve. Don't expect your child to be a star athlete or an "A" student if he or she lacks given ability. The expectations should not be based on what you have expected of older siblings or children of your friends or relatives. Setting goals beyond the child's ability can result in discouragement, failure and a lack of motivation, so base your expectations on what you feel is realistic for the individual child. This is especially important if your child is having difficulty in school or in particular areas important to him or her.

The expectations you set come from the dreams, hopes, and long-range goals you have for your child. It is important to share these dreams, hopes and goals so your child understands how you feel about his or her capabilities. The kinds of expectations you set might relate to how well you expect your child to do in school, the level of musical ability you believe she has, or the kinds of athletic skills you believe can be attained. They might also relate to the kind of person you would like your child to become. This is why it is important that you decide on the characteristics you feel are most vital.

ॐ ॐ ॐ

When you discuss these expectations with your child, leave room for negotiation. It's important that your child agree with you on what is reasonable. It also helps to express your expectations in general rather than specific terms or specific accomplishments. One way to do this is to discuss areas where you feel your child can grow or improve. For example, you might ask him or her to improve in reading or to increase computational speed in math, without specifying the exact level you expect.

An effective way to express expectations is in the form of challenges. For example, you might ask your child, "Do you think you can get four more words correct on your spelling test this week?" or state, "Let's see if you can perform this task in just 30 minutes instead of an hour," or "I'd like to see you improve in this subject." This provides a challenge for the child yet allows some leeway. Challenges can reduce fear of failure yet stimulate the desire to achieve. Challenges also are easier to modify if it appears you have set your sights too high.

Remember, self-motivation is the long-term goal and your child needs to participate in setting expectations in areas they value so it is appropriate to ask the child to initiate discussions on how he can improve performance. In helping your child develop a sense of identity be sure you have explored his interests and aptitudes. Likewise, work towards agreement on expectations you both feel are realistic and relevant. Listen to your child. Take his ideas seriously. Ask him what hopes and dreams he has for his future.

೧೯ ೧೯ ೧೯

Expand your child's interests and comfort zone

Children become highly motivated when they have new experiences. Introduce them to new hobbies, new games, and new opportunities to explore subjects or objects with which they are not familiar. Learning a new skill, exploring a new experience, and stimulating curiosity regarding a new subject can all be effective ways of increasing the level of motivation. A prerequisite to this is creating an atmosphere where it becomes emotionally safe to risk and where the emphasis is on trying things out. This means not making fun of them when they don't succeed. Begin expanding your children's interests and talents by sharing your own passions and interests. If possible let them join in your pursuits and talk about why they are important to you.

Develop your child's artistic senses and appreciation for art and music. Point out sights or scenes you appreciate for their beauty or a sense of peace. Bob attributes his strong sense of wonder and appreciation for nature, including butterflies, flowers, fall colors, sunsets, and scenery, to his grandmother, who always expressed her sense of wonder about nature when he was young. She was so passionate about it that she wrote poems to express her feelings. Her passion and wonder was infectious. Attend a concert or an art exhibit together with your child. Such an experience can inspire a child to take up a musical instrument or desire to draw or paint. Bob recalls being motivated to take up a musical instrument after attending his first symphony concert when he was age 9, an activity he still enjoys.

When your child seems bored or bogged down here are some things you might try to expand his or her interests and comfort zone:

- ◆ Provide opportunities to visit the zoo to stimulate an interest in animals and how they live.
- ◆ Visit a factory or workplace.
- ◆ Stimulate your child with information on new subjects.
- ◆ Visit a point of historical interest.
- ◆ Talk with someone involved in interesting work.
- ◆ Take in an art show or concert.
- ◆ Explore a new game to play.
- ◆ Encourage your child to watch educational programs such as those put on by *National Geographic* on animals or different countries.

ॐ ॐ ॐ

Provide your child with different materials with which to work. These materials might include tools, cooking ingredients, new computer programs, art supplies, sewing materials, or a new magazine or book to read. By encouraging your child to develop new interests or hobbies, opportunities for him or her to learn new skills are increased. Even though some of these interests may be short lived, children build new skills, interests, and knowledge with each one. Learn together and try out new experiences with your child so you become a role model.

ॐ ॐ ॐ

Sometimes parents wonder whether it is worth investing in a child's expressed interest like a musical instrument, piano, judo or skating lessons or some other interest that involves an expense on their part. One guiding principle is to get your child to agree to make some form of commitment to match your expenditure of funds. This might mean contributing some of her own funds or committing to staying with that interest for a given period of time, perhaps a month or six weeks. You may want to require your child to help you out in exchange for the time commitment required on your part. At the end of that agreed upon time period you can then decide whether it is worth making a heavier investment. In general, it's usually worth the time and expense at least to respond to your child's expressed interest in any new endeavor.

Each of us has a comfort zone, where we know what to expect and where we function comfortably. Unfortunately, some individuals never expand that comfort zone. Consequently, whenever these individuals are faced with change or a new situation their level of stress increases significantly. One fact of life is that the world of the future will be full of changes. Encourage your children to test out new situations so they become accustomed to change:

- ◆ Encourage them to risk learning something new.
- ◆ Have them develop one new skill.
- ◆ Encourage them to engage in speaking before a group.
- ◆ Have them spend time with individuals from different cultures.
- ◆ Introduce them to different foods.
- ◆ Try to go to new places.
- ◆ Both you and your children try to learn a different language.

༄ ༄ ༄

When your children have taken the courage to risk or expose themselves to a new experience, make certain you acknowledge them for their courage, regardless of whether they feel they were successful or not. Once exposed to a wide variety of situations, children are more likely to feel more comfortable in different settings where they may have to function in unfamiliar ways.

By expanding your children's interests you are creating a stimulating environment that will open up opportunities for learning, a chance to gain new friends and most important of all, you are likely to increase their general level of motivation.

Some activities to consider:

1. Encourage your children to try one new skill, investigate one new interest, meet with a different group, try a different food, seek out a new friend, or read different kind of book at least once each month.

2. Have your child identify one skill or talent he would like to develop that you could help with. Then plan the best way to go about this.

3. Expose your child to successful people. Tell her about individuals who have made a great contribution. Check biographies out of the library to read with your child or have her read herself. Talk about the traits that made these people successful or great.

Develop values to live by

A motivating factor in children's lives is the desire to become the kind of people they believe their parents want. This requires that you communicate clearly the values and personal characteristics you believe are most important. This might include honesty, concern and caring for others, respect for seniors, reliability, tolerance of those different from oneself, initiative, love of nature, environmental sensitivity, and a sense of patriotism.

Talk with your children about the values that were important to you when you were growing up, and which values are most dear to you now. Which values serve as guides for the way you live your life? Of course it is most important for you to model those values and "walk the talk." Children can spot hypocrisy in a heartbeat!

For younger children, it's easy to find books where the major characters in the story model particular characteristics. Another strategy is to have your children identify role models or individuals they truly admire. Unfortunately, so many of their heroes have traits that are not at all admirable. Some athletes, for example, can be overly self-centered or inarticulate, and are therefore poor examples. Other poor models include the football hero who ends up in jail for drug or spousal abuse, or the rock star who models clothes on TV that most parents would not allow their daughter to wear outside their home. However, these athletes might be admired for their determination, courage, or dedication. When you have your children select their favorite heroes or heroines, have them identify what particular qualities they value in these individuals. Ask them if they believe they have some of these same qualities. Ask which qualities they would like to develop in themselves. Since September the 11th, 2001, children often name firemen or policemen or soldiers because of their courage. Sometimes, it's Dad or Mom, and quite often it's a grandparent!

ඉංඥ ඉංඥ ඉංඥ

Resiliency is one of those traits that is admirable in children and adults—the ability to overcome adversity and rise above difficulties or circumstances. To encourage children to value resiliency, read to them stories of people like Wilma Rudolph or Lance Armstrong, people who overcame adversity and became heroes. The movie *Chariots of Fire* is also inspirational, as it concerns the two English track stars who won medals in the Olympics—one motivated by a desire to spread God's message of peace and the other by his need to combat anti-Semitism.

Passion and commitment to ideals are values that many parents would like to see in their children. Because children learn best by observing your behavior, such values are best communicated by modeling your own passion for causes, for hobbies or interests, or for helping others. Encourage your children to feel passionate about their interests and to become fully engaged in those activities. Talk with them about those causes you feel strongly about, and help them understand why these causes are important to you. This will encourage your children to develop strong positions and commitment to their own ideals.

Are you concerned about your children's obsession with material possessions—wishing for the latest video game, the latest style shoes or clothes, or a new toy that has just come on the market? This is a common problem in many families. One way to foster fiscal responsibility and delayed gratification is to take your child shopping with you when you have no intention of buying the item right then, or possibly ever. For example, take the children with you while you look at the latest TV or the new RV's. Explain that you don't have enough money now to purchase something like that, but you are just doing your homework, checking on prices, and determining how much you would have to save before you could get something like that. This way, your children will realize that usually we don't get everything we want, but it is okay to look and dream.

⌘ ⌘ ⌘

Some activities to consider:

1. After watching a TV show or movie, talk with your children about personal qualities they admire in the characters they have just seen. Select characters that might serve as good role models, and have your children talk about the ways in which they are like those individuals.

2. Talk with your children about the significance of having a good reputation. Discuss the benefits that could come from that. Then discuss how quickly that reputation can be destroyed.

3. Have your children identify some specific values they try to live by. Ask them how they came to feel that these were important values. Share some of your values, and talk about where those values came from in your life.

ॐ ॐ ॐ

Most children question how they fit into this world and what place they have in it. Some feel alone and don't see the relationship between themselves and anything greater than themselves. This can be depressing and disturbing. Human beings are spiritual by nature, though that doesn't necessarily mean religious. Spirituality is an active identification with things greater than oneself, things that give life meaning and purpose. Having such a connection or a belief in something larger than oneself offers children a sense of significance and possibilities of support. Children are likely to feel comforted and happier when they feel a spiritual relationship with a divine power, whether it be God, Goddess, Mind, the Source, Universal Energy, or some other form of Higher Power.

ॐ ॐ ॐ

Such spirituality is based on the concept of an underlying, indwelling creative force that infuses all of life, including ourselves, and makes us connected to all of nature and the universe. You might convey to your children that there seems to be a master plan for the universe, and that they are part of that master plan. Children need to see beauty in virtually every object they see. They need to see the goodness inherent in all people. They need to think of the world as good, positive, and something to be valued. Joan Chittister, author and director of Benetvision—a resource center for spirituality—expressed it this way: "The spirituality we develop is the filter through which we view our worlds and the limits in which we operate."

ॐ ॐ ॐ

The seeds of spirituality can be planted early in children's lives, developing as they mature. You can help your children experience feelings of spirituality by discussing with them your own beliefs. You can develop their spiritual relationship by praying or worshipping with them, by jointly experiencing the joy of music, by helping them to pray or meditate, or by helping them strive for a productive life and seeing their role as fulfilling a part of a larger plan or purpose. This spiritual connection can also be furthered by helping them experience the satisfaction that comes from contributing to a group effort for the good of others. Sharing concerns about the welfare of others and engaging in efforts to make life better for them, especially for those who are in greater need than themselves, again helps children develop this sense of purpose.

Build a vision of the future

Talk with your children about the future; this can add to their motivation. Discuss with them how the world they will inhabit as an adult might differ and/or be similar to what it is now. Many children either have a distorted view of the future or don't think about the future at all. When asked what their vision of the future might be, many are likely to think in terms of space ships or some fantasy world. Explore various scenarios with your child. Discuss the kind of changes you have seen in your lifetime, and speculate on the changes likely to have taken place by the time they get out of school. Be sure also to talk about things that are likely to remain the same, so they understand that their world will be fundamentally similar to how the world is today. Let them know how you feel about them going to college, and about the importance of education in the world of tomorrow. Create a vision of greatness in your children that can become a consuming drive for achievement! Convey what role you hope to see them play in the future. Discuss strengths you see in them and how they might make effective use of those strengths as an adult. While they are still in elementary school, take them for a visit to a college campus—those images can provide a strong motivating force.

Thinking about the future can begin by having your child learn to transcend immediate personal wants and be willing to delay gratification, which we have mentioned earlier. Help him become less focused on his immediate wants and more interested in adopting a long-range perspective. This might mean saving his money for something really worthwhile, having ambitions regarding the kind of person he wants to become and the kind of work he would like to do. Encourage your child to think about contributions she believes she could make, what she might like to discover or develop, or what problem she believes she could solve.

అశ్ అశ్ అశ్

Children need to believe they have some control over their lives. Encourage your children to take on the role of a social activist in their own world. This can be as simple as establishing the habit of picking up litter in their neighborhood. Encourage them to become involved in student government at school, make suggestions to their principal, write a letter to the mayor, or work for causes they deem admirable. Be their role model or point out others who make a difference. Remind them of Margaret Mead, who said, "Never doubt that a small group of thoughtful, committed citizens can change the world; indeed, it's the only thing that ever has."

అశ్ అశ్ అశ్

Even at an early age, children can think about what they want to accomplish. Try talking with preschool children about what they plan to build with blocks or what they plan to paint. Then follow it up by asking if they were pleased with the results or how they might do it differently next time to make it better. In general, the younger the child, the shorter or smaller the goal should be. As children grow older, they should be able to set longer range goals, developing the habit of being clear about what they are doing and what they should get out of it. They should know the skills they want to strengthen, ways in which they would like to change, or things they would like to be able to do for themselves. Share goals or dreams you have for yourself, so your child begins to understand that setting goals for oneself is a natural thing to do.

When your child has decided on an important goal, it may be important to get a commitment to reach that goal. For older children it helps to have them put this in writing so you can refer to it from time to time if necessary. It's important to discuss what resources they will need and to set some benchmarks along the way, as well as determining a way to evaluate completion of the goal. Have your child commit to sticking with the goal until it is achieved or until you both agree that it should be revised or dropped. It often helps to establish a date for completion of the goal.

When you work with your child to set a goal, as a parent, you have the responsibility to provide the kind of support he might need to achieve that goal. Have your child clarify the role that he would like for you to play and what you might do to help.

ॐ ॐ ॐ

Demonstrate faith and confidence in your child's ability to succeed

Children, especially those who lack confidence in themselves, are likely to believe they are incapable of achieving the goals that have been set unless you first convince them that you believe they can accomplish those goals. Many of us have achieved goals we felt were impossible only because someone else believed we could do it. For some children, just cleaning their rooms may seem to be completely overwhelming and out of the realm of possibility. When you have faith in your child's ability and your child knows this, your child is much more likely to put forth extra effort to achieve the goals that have been set. For particularly difficult tasks, you may need to provide extra support and reassurance until your child becomes convinced that the goal can be achieved. In most instances, you will find that your child keeps trying as long as you believe in his ability to succeed.

In some cases, a mentor can convey this confidence. For example, Karen was a 17-year-old girl who might alarm you if you saw her on the street. Her hair was dyed green; she had tattoos on each arm; and she had pierced her face with a ring and studs. She lived on the street and slept at night in an old banged-up car with her mother in downtown Seattle. However, she had a mother who believed in her and a teacher in high school who served as her mentor. Her mother encouraged her to take up a musical instrument, so she learned to play violin in the school orchestra. When she considered dropping out of school because she couldn't afford to go to college, her teacher conveyed faith in her and encouraged her to remain and apply for a college scholarship. She did graduate from high school, and to the surprise of many received a full, four-year scholarship to Harvard University—all because these two individuals believed in her!

"Put it under something."

Many adults have achieved fame and fortune only as a result of the encouragement they received from others. So create a vision of greatness in your child that will serve to inspire her and encourage her to strive to be the best she can be.

Some activities to consider:

1. Have your children draw a picture of the house they hope to live in as an adult and/or talk about the kind of equipment they would like to have in the house.

2. Explore with your children some of the inventions and current explorations that may have implications for their life and their work in the future. Talk about the kinds of skills they may need to succeed in the future.

3. When your child sets out to achieve a goal, be certain to check with him regarding the kind of support he believes he needs from you and the role he wants you to play in the process.

Summary

Set expectations for your children and let them know of your hopes and dreams for them. Encourage them to consider their future so they have reason to do well in school, work to become the person they wish to be, and be motivated in all they do. By clarifying your expectations, strengthening your family values, building their self-confidence, encouraging them to pursue meaningful goals, and then supporting their efforts to achieve those goals you can contribute significantly to their motivation and sense of purpose.

Chapter 7
Key #5: Building a Sense
of Personal Competence

*"There are countless ways of attaining greatness, but any road
to reaching one's maximum potential must be built on a bedrock
of respect for the individual, a commitment to excellence,
and a rejection of mediocrity."*

Buck Rogers

ૐ ૐ ૐ

The fifth key is building a "sense of personal competence." Having a sense of personal competence is critical to feelings of self-confidence, resilience, and independence. Feelings of competence enable children to feel confident in their ability to deal with whatever life brings. It's the belief that they possess the personal power, skills required, and knowledge of how to access resources to deal with any problems, issues, and challenges they might face. It comes through multiple experiences and successes and might be defined as "quiet confidence in one's potential"— not necessarily having all the answers but confident in being able to reach eventual success in spite of one's shortcomings.

A natural context for developing personal competence is helping children achieve goals they have set. This provides a context for applying problem solving skills, decision-making skills, use of resources, assessing growth, and determining success.

Develop positive and productive attitudes

Children should be taught that they always have a choice in how they deal with what happens to them. They can either choose to be miserable, unhappy, and give up, or they can choose to be happy and try to make the best of their situation. Encouraging your child to choose a positive approach to circumstances not only leads to more happiness, it also contributes to better health. Medical experts testify that those with a positive attitude have less stress and are less susceptible to illnesses and diseases, and that a positive mental attitude is a better predictor of health than any other medical risk factor. As in the song sung by Lee Ann Womack, "When given the choice, I hope you choose to dance!"

ॐ ॐ ॐ

When children seek to achieve their dreams or to work on their goals, it's likely that they might not succeed at first. It is important for children to learn to cope with defeat or perceived failures. When your child undertakes a goal it is seldom a matter of failing or succeeding. No one likes to fail, but you can teach your child a healthy way to view "failure." Point out to children the numerous benefits of trying, even if he doesn't completely succeed. In the process of trying he may gain new skills, a new way of approaching things, new friends, knowledge of new resources, or achieve something he didn't expect.

Get your children to think about the growth they are making. For example, if they view their effort as growing in experience or insight rather than succeeding or failing, they can focus on what it might take for them to achieve success next time, or the time after that. It has been demonstrated over time that the most successful people in life actually fail more frequently than others. This is true in sports, in business, and in life. Usually it's necessary to try over and over again.

Another way of looking at progress toward a goal is to think of a sailboat. A sailboat is off course about 90% of the time, but it is always correcting its course because its captain knows where he is trying to go. Help your child remember what she wants to accomplish, and encourage her to keep at it until she succeeds. This is how persistence is fostered.

One of the most important things you can do as a parent is to model how to deal with frustration and disappointment. Parents who display a lack of temper control when they are frustrated often forget that they are serving as models for their children. You want to be a positive rather than a negative model in this. Share with your child what you are trying to do, how you are going about it and how you deal with things when they don't work out right. This creates an important model for behavior and will leave a greater impression on your child than anything you can say.

Dr. Prigogene, the Nobel Prize winner, received his award for developing the "Theory of Dissipative Structures." He was able to prove that microorganisms, as well as other animals, actually reconstitute themselves as a higher form of life when undergoing stress. Thus, it is possible that when children are feeling a great deal of stress, they may actually be learning new skills and new perspectives or insights that will enable them to deal with that situation in the future without feeling the same level of stress. Have your children consider the beginning of the school year and how stressful that was at one time. Now they hardly even give going to school a thought. This can be true for most other situations that they find stressful at first.

"Could you please put my mom on his do-not-call list?"

Let mistakes happen. Children need to learn from their mistakes and failures. Use their failures or mistakes as opportunities to help them grow and become wiser.

Some activities to consider:

1. Establish the habit of ending the day by sharing with your children what went well today and what they are looking forward to for tomorrow.

2. Have children develop an ongoing list of "Smart Things To Do" as they learn of smart ways to act, respond, think, or feel. Include significant ideas they learn from school, from books, from others, or through insights that they come up with themselves.

3. Post inspiring quotations or sayings in your child's room or on the refrigerator as reminders.

4. When your children are working on a difficult task, have them record what they learned from each attempt or each stage, so they can profit from and see growth from that experience.

Explore options and alternatives with your child

When your child sets a goal, one of the first things you can do is to help clarify the problem or goal on which he wishes to work. Ask him questions so he can share how he perceives the situation, what might need to be changed, and what hurdles or barriers are likely to appear. Brainstorm possible options or alternative ways he might approach the problem. Allow your child to choose one option or alternative solution after considering all the various possibilities and implications—one he believes will solve the problem. Let him feel good about the solution. The goal may even be something difficult to measure. For example, the goal may be to develop personal traits that help him become a better person. This may be a goal he continually works on and never completely achieves, but the same processes can apply.

After working with a number of children using this process, we are surprised at how children often take an approach quite different from one an adult would have taken. Sometimes this is because they would rather work with one of their friends on the problem than do it alone, or because they don't believe they have a particular skill that might be required, even when we think they do. That's why you need to give the child primary responsibility for deciding which option to use.

Part of achieving success in any endeavor relates to the effective use of resources. Teaching children where to go for help and what resources can be used to attain goals contributes to becoming competent. As your child identifies areas where she might need help, teach her how she can access information and how to use various references in a library or the Internet. Parents who teach their children effective use of the dictionary, almanac, encyclopedia, reference section of the library, and how to access information on the Internet do their children a great favor.

If your child decides to work on developing a personal quality such as being more cheerful or having more friends, point out mentors, relatives, or friends that can guide and help your child. It may be that just observing others can be a valuable source of information. Your child might also find some answers in self-help books or in seeking the opinion or advice of other respected adults. The important thing for the child is to realize that there are lots of options.

✺ ✺ ✺

Research indicates that having a mentor, other than a parent, can be a great resource and a positive influence, especially for adolescents. This is a time when children want to appear grown up to their parents, so they may be reluctant to share their concerns; yet they may be open to the opinion or advice of another adult. It might be helpful, therefore, to suggest another adult your child can go to for advice or assistance with different kinds of problems.

Help children solve problems independently

To acquire the sense of personal competence, children need to learn how to solve problems on their own, how to make decisions for themselves, and how to profit from their mistakes. It is usually easier for us as parents or grandparents to help children solve their problems than it is to see them struggle to find the answers on their own. But children who become dependent on their parents or others feel helpless and resentful rather than competent. It is a mistake to make excuses for them, bail them out of difficulties, or step in to solve problems they should be able to solve on their own. When you do, they are apt to internalize the message, "You are not able to handle yourself and you need adults to help you." As a result, many children continue to behave irresponsibly, resent authority figures, and feel inadequate. However, you can be a significant help in enabling your children to solve problems on their own by allowing them to struggle on their own sometimes.

๛ ๛ ๛

As children mature, they need to learn a problem-solving/decision-making process that will help them make appropriate choices. Help them use a process such as this in planning or problem solving:

1. Define the problem or question.

2. List the possible options or choices available.

3. Envision the possible consequences for each (short-and-long term).

4. Consider two questions:
   ◆ What would I advise my best friend to do in this situation?
   ◆ What would the person I want to become choose to do?

5. Make a decision and assume responsibility for the consequences.

By following such processes as these you are helping your child grow in her ability to solve problems and make decisions on her own.

> ## Some activities to consider:
>
> 1. Teach your children different ways to solve problems: through negotiation or trade off, through compromise, by taking turns, or working together. As examples, use problems such as conflicts over TV, games to play, chores to be done, use of the telephone, or invading privacy.
>
> 2. Use a recent example of one of your child's experiences to apply the "what, why, how" process.
>
> 3. Encourage your young child to make choices and then experience the outcome of those choices. Explain cause and effect to your child.

‰ ‰ ‰

Develop the skills of good judgment

Children need to receive guidance and training in how to use their judgment skills. You have a significant impact on choices your child makes until about the age of ten, but after age ten other forces come into play. By the middle of adolescence, your child will have been exposed to thousands of messages from peers, magazines, movies, radio, and TV. Not all of these messages are in your child's best interests. Thus, it is important to teach your child to say "Yes" to a life of accountability, "Yes" to healthy life choices, and "No" to those options that are not in his best long-term interests.

Using good judgment requires that children have a set of values or guidelines on which to base decisions. They need to learn about and understand the values that you as the parent use in making your decisions as well as those commonly held by society. They need to learn how to treat others and how they wish to be treated. As they become older, children need to understand the concepts of justice and what is morally right. As they begin to grasp these concepts, you need to ask them, "What would be the 'right' thing to do in this case?" and "What leads you to believe this is the 'right' thing to do?"

ॐ ॐ ॐ

Avoid the tendency to lecture, instruct, direct, moralize, or even dictate what the 'right' thing to do is, but help your children think through their position and what it is based on. Generally, situations will have more than a simple answer, more than one position that could be taken. Your objective is to help your child learn to think through her position and justify it.

ॐ ॐ ॐ

Children are often inclined to base their decisions on what their peers would do. Unfortunately, this can sometimes lead to disastrous circumstances. Peers often are likely to tell their friends what they should do without evaluating that choice against any criteria or set of values. Peers may even encourage friends to do things they wouldn't do themselves, sometimes just to see what might happen. A common example is encouraging someone else to throw a rock through a window. Although some children wouldn't do such a thing themselves, they will encourage someone else to try it so they can later say, "I wasn't the one that threw the rock."

ॐ ॐ ॐ

Engage in dialogue with your child about hypothetical as well as real situations. This provides practice in making judgment decisions before a real situation occurs. In some cases it is even helpful to role-play a situation and discuss with your child possible consequences of a decision or position. Once your child has grown accustomed to analyzing decisions and thinking through possible consequences, both you and your child will begin to have greater confidence in the decisions made.

Some activities to consider:

1. Have your child identify possible dilemmas he could be facing at school, such as gaining friends, playing with others, being tempted by a close friend, or having to make a decision about his life. Talk about how he might go about making the right decision, what he would use as criteria, or whom he could go to for advice.

2. Discuss approaches your child might take when faced with a personal conflict between her own wishes, desires, and values and how she can best arrive at a solution. Have her share a decision she recently made that makes her feel proud.

3. Discuss with your child the various bases on which to make a decision— e.g. various teachings, the Bible, his personal values, your advice or values, legal laws or rules, advice of friends, his inner intuition of what is right, what his peers are doing.

4. It is just as important to help your child think about the results of generous and considerate behavior as it is to consider the results of inconsiderate behavior.

One way of helping your children make more appropriate decisions is to use what is sometimes referred to as the "What? Why? How?" process. Talk with your child about his successes and failures by helping him answer these questions:

1. Describe the experience you just had.

2. Identify what was significant about that experience. What happened? How did you feel? What did you learn?

3. Why do you think this happened? What caused it to turn out like it did? What did you do or not do that caused it to turn out that way?

4. How might you want to deal with this situation next time?

How could you do it differently? What do you think would be the outcome? What option or choice will you make next time?

In this way, you can use your child's experience as a teaching or learning experience to help him develop the practice of analyzing what happened, what he did to cause it to happen, and how he can deal with it in the future. This helps him profit from his own mistakes or so-called failures. It also stresses the fact that he is usually going to be held accountable for the decisions he makes.

ଚଚ ଚଚ ଚଚ

Monitor their choices and progress

As a parent, your role is not to direct as much as it is to help your children develop the ability to make sound and healthy choices. After your child has made a decision, it is usually wise for you to check to see whether she is headed in the proper direction before it is too late. For example, she may decide she would like to work on a project with a friend or do her homework on the floor in the living room. However, it may become evident that not much progress is being made, so it may be well to suggest that she explore another option.

Children often need help measuring their progress or determining when they have actually reached what they set out to do. It helps when they can define this before they start, but they often need adult feedback or observations to determine their progress. You can help your children track progress by first having them write down what they really hope to accomplish. Then have them identify what obstacles can be foreseen or what adjustments might be necessary. At completion, have them compare these ideas with what has been accomplished.

Benchmarks or ways you and your child are able to monitor progress can be valuable in two ways:

1. They enable you to keep informed regarding the progress made.

2. Benchmarks can often serve as a motivating device.

Benchmarks are one way you and your child can monitor progress. They can help you track the progress being made and they can also serve as a motivating force. When a child can measure progress by noting steps mastered, he is more likely to be motivated to advance to the next step. For example, in mathematics the addition, subtraction, or multiplication tables are easily divided into stages so the child is encouraged to master one stage at a time. Other benchmarks might be to use report card grades each quarter, to record and monitor test results, or to keep a portfolio of work over a period of time to note improvements. However, in most areas your child may need to rely on your observations and feedback.

"Sure it's fun, but it doesn't give me a feeling of accomplishment."

Provide ongoing support and encouragement

Most children begin working on their goals with great enthusiasm, but this wanes as they become frustrated and bogged down. To overcome this, a vital role you as a parent can perform is to provide that note of encouragement. To illustrate the importance of encouragement, you can relate the story of Florence Chadwick, the famous swimmer. It was reported that several years ago Florence Chadwick set out to swim from Catalina Island to the mainland by Los Angeles, a distance of some 28 miles.

After she had been in the water 14 hours and had been stung twice by sting rays, the fog came in and she couldn't see where she was. She decided to give up and had the people in the boat that was accompanying lift her into the boat . When they headed for shore she was only a few hundred yards from her goal of 28 miles. She reported that if they had told her how far she had come, she knew she could have made it!

There are times when children need to see how far they have come and how little they need to do to accomplish their goal. Use the benchmarks they have met to indicate progress they have made. By encouraging them, you are building their ability to persevere under difficulty, which is an important adult skill.

When your child experiences great frustration, disappointment, or crisis, this is the time to validate her feelings and emphasize your love and support. Post inspirational quotations or posters around her room to encourage her. After the crisis has passed, discuss with her what she has learned from the experience or how she might profit from it. This can often be helpful knowledge in making a second effort or in overcoming frustrations or failures in the future.

Some activities to consider:

1. Make an ongoing list of skills your child has learned or things he can now do what he couldn't do before.

2. As your child's birthday approaches, make a list of all the improvements or accomplishments that you have noticed from the previous year and ways in which she has grown. Then present that to her as a gift or as something to post in her room.

3. Have your child prepare a timeline marking all the significant things he has achieved in his lifetime. Have him mark his timeline with things he hopes to achieve in the future.

Celebrate success

When your child has accomplished what he set out to do, this is a magical moment and should be a time of great significance. This might be learning how to dress himself, finishing a model, learning the multiplication tables, reading a book, or making a goal on the soccer team. Your child needs to internalize the thrill of being successful. When he has an opportunity to share his feelings of success with other members of the family, and family members support those feelings, the celebration can be a source of motivation to advance to bigger things. However, if his achievements are belittled or discounted it can also discourage further efforts along this line.

ॐ ॐ ॐ

Most children, like adults, are motivated by rewards of one kind or another. One way to use rewards is in connection with the goals your child has set. Younger children enjoy working with checklists or charts on which they can get a star or sticker or some form of recognition. Completing a checklist or getting a certain number of stars might result in the child having her favorite dinner, the privilege of selecting a movie to see, or special time with you. All children value the opportunity to do something special as a reward—make a cake, go to a movie, make popcorn, have dinner out, spend a day at the park, go to a ball game, build a tree house, or go camping. Activities that involve you are the most rewarding for children, as well as giving you the chance to enjoy fun activities with your child. And because the fun event is occurring as a result of your child's effort, it makes the child feel even more special.

In addition to rewards, the pleasure that comes from making others happy, the thrill of competition, the challenge of self-improvement, and the satisfaction of a job well done, there are other forms of motivation. As children mature, they should become motivated by their own sense of satisfaction and growth rather than by material rewards.

The moment of success is like magic because it usually reinforces the other elements you have been building. When children see themselves as successful, they are likely to feel more secure. The experience of success is likely to change how they see themselves, encouraging them to set higher goals for themselves by examining how they could build on their success. As children use what they have learned to achieve even higher goals, the cycle repeats itself and internal motivation begins to grow. From that point you, as a parent, are likely to take the role of encouraging, coaching, and supporting instead of directing, correcting, and pushing.

Children who experience enough successful experiences begin to acquire a wide variety of alternative strategies for solving problems and accomplishing objectives. They become resourceful and more likely to become internally motivated and independent. Developing this state of being in your child should be one of your more significant objectives. It is one of the joys of parenting!

ॐ ॐ ॐ

Summary

Competence comes about as a result of accomplishing goals or tasks that are challenging for us. It comes about over time. Parents can assist in this process by teaching their children effective use of resources, by monitoring the progress children make as a result of their choices, by providing ongoing support, by offering feedback to help children evaluate their goals, and finally by celebrating children's successes. The object of this phase is to develop self-motivation as well as reinforce positive self-images.

Chapter 8
Helping Children
with Unique Needs

KIDS WHO ARE DIFFERENT
Here's to the kids who are different,
The kids who don't always get A's,
The kids who have ears
twice the size of their peers,
And noses that go on for days...
Here's to the kids who are different,
The kids they call crazy or dumb,
The kids who don't fit,
with the guts and the grit
Who dance to a different drum...
Here's to the kids who are different,
The kids with the mischievous streak,
For when they have grown,
as history's shown,
It's their difference that makes them unique.

Author Unknown

ॐ ॐ ॐ

Every child is unique. The parenting style used with one child may not be appropriate for another, even in the same family. Often unique problems become barriers to children in reaching their potential. Parents who are aware of the problems that can develop from circumstances beyond their control are able to take steps to compensate for these problems, because most problems are not insurmountable and can be overcome in a loving, accepting environment.

ॐ ॐ ॐ

Temperament/personality

Most parents will tell you that personality is something that was present at birth. If they have more than one child, they will also be able to inform you how different their little sweethearts are from each other. Some children are consistently sunny and optimistic from day one. Others are inconsistent and mercurial; they keep you guessing by waking up one morning with a smile and hug and the next day with a scowl. A growing body of research shows that newborns express their emotional makeup early. According to Lawrence Diller, professor of pediatrics at the University of California, San Francisco, this could give parents a chance to take control of behavior problems before they fully take hold. Diller believes that we can match our parenting style to the child's personality and improve the situation for both parents and child.

In the 1950s, the team of Stella Chase and Alexander Thomas identified the following nine parameters of temperament:

- ◆ activity level
- ◆ attention span
- ◆ adaptability
- ◆ intensity
- ◆ distractibility
- ◆ mood
- ◆ sensory threshold
- ◆ response to challenge
- ◆ predictability of function

According to Chase and Thomas, these behaviors are discernible at one month. Although these findings were dismissed at the time they were published, practitioners today are finding new relevance in this old work. Behavioral scientists today have found that 60% of babies have easy temperaments from birth, while most of the rest exhibit moodiness, defiance, or other traits that place them in the difficult category. These scientists believe that, without intervention, 80% of these "difficult" children will act out, become oppositional and hyper-excitable, and run a greater risk of developing ADHD (Attention Deficit Hyperactivity Disorder). The remaining 20%, mostly girls, become withdrawn and run a greater risk of developing phobias, depressions or compulsions. Of course not every child in the difficult group will follow this course.

✌ ✌ ✌

Temperament is your child's behavioral style. Often, if we don't understand our child's temperament, we are inclined to blame ourselves or the child for situations or feelings that are perfectly normal for that child. If, on the other hand, we understand the temperament, we can plan effective strategies to deal with those situations and feelings. We know that both energy level and adjustability are partially inherited, but we also know that both can be influenced by environment and parenting style.

✌ ✌ ✌

The key to prevention lies in effective parenting, and in realizing that what works with one child may not work with another. For example, if your child resists new experiences, slowly expose the child to the idea and gradually introduce him to the new experience. Children who are fearful of "what might happen if" should be helped to anticipate the "what ifs" and talk about how they could handle the possible happenings, so they feel secure and prepared. Temperament is related to how your child will learn. A child who has an active, fast adjusting temperament will learn more by doing and practicing, while a quieter, slower adjusting child will learn more by observing and internally rehearsing. Your child's personality and temperament are unique and part of his/her individuality. Some personalities and temperaments are more challenging than others but, once understood, can be helped by adapting your parenting style to meet the needs of your challenging child.

Gender issues

From an early age, most young boys play and behave differently than young girls; so it is only natural for parents to believe that gender differences are innate and biological. Many researchers in the past have argued that it's in the genes or it's in the environment. The nurture-nature pendulum of belief has swung back and forth. Today, scientists generally agree that gender-specific behavior is a mixture of the two.

Many of the behavioral differences between boys and girls may lie in the eye of the beholder. Television certainly reinforces the stereotypical perception. Parents, too, especially fathers, tend to reinforce gender roles by choosing toys that are gender specific. Parents tend to talk more to their daughters, give them less autonomy, and encourage them to play a helping role when interacting with others. On the other hand, parents encourage sons to express some emotions but not others (like fearfulness).

ᏜᎬ ᏜᎬᎰ ᏜᎬ

By the time children are school age, boys often feel the need to suppress emotions that are considered feminine. They feel peer pressure to conform and "fit in," and they are caught up in meeting the expectations of others. They are sometimes bullied because they are considered too feminine or too "nerdy." Girls, on the other hand, believe they must choose between being intelligent and being popular. Studies by the AAUW show that girls become "voiceless," choosing not to express their opinions and ideas, often withholding the "right answers" in class, for fear of being labeled smart! Their identity, at least in the Caucasian culture, is their body image. As a result, eating disorders are common in young teenage girls.

What can parents do? Experts argue that parents can provide their children with a range of experiences that go beyond the stereotypical. Claire Etaugh, co-director of the Bradley University Center for the Study of Early Childhood Development, offers this important insight: "By giving children opportunities to participate in all kinds of activities, you're going to wind up with children who have the freedom to choose what they're good at and like doing."

In raising boys, validate the belief that it's okay to have emotions and encourage boys to express those emotions to people they trust. Listen, empathize, and explain the dilemma of gender stereotyping and societal expectations. Be aware of the stress and overload male children may be experiencing. Encourage your son to follow his own interests, and help him find same interest-based groups or individuals.

In raising girls, provide positive female role models. Parents of girls need to help their children find their identity and interest as early as possible. Emphasize that identity is who we are, not what we look like, and that body health is more important than body image. Validate the idea that women can have career and life choices and can enjoy a balance of roles. Girls need to know that assertive behavior is not aggressive behavior. They need to be encouraged to have control over their lives by accepting the idea that intelligence is valued and the use of intelligence is power. Listen seriously to their ideas and beliefs, and involve them in decision-making.

Experts suggest that parents should not push their children into gender-typical behavior and activities, but should instead trust their instincts and be supportive about what their children are doing. Most of all, as a parent you should be your child's model and mentor.

છૠ ૭૭ છૠ

ADHD

At one time or another, all children have trouble being attentive; but when it occurs consistently and over a long period of time, children may be considered to have Attention Deficit Disorder (ADD). If they also have difficulty sitting still without fidgeting, they may have Attention Deficit Hyperactivity Disorder (ADHD). This disorder is a syndrome that interferes with an individual's ability to focus (inattention), regulate activity level (hyperactivity), and inhibit behavior (impulsivity). It is one of the most common learning disorders in children and adolescents, and the incidence in children appears to be increasing.

Research tells us that this syndrome affects about two to three times more boys than girls. ADHD becomes evident in preschool or elementary school, frequently persisting into adolescence and occasionally into adulthood. There is no specific test for ADHD. The diagnosis results from a review of a physical examination, a variety of psychological tests, and observable behaviors in everyday settings. If you suspect that your child may have ADD or ADHD, you can use a behavioral checklist for observable behaviors often supplied by the doctor. Listed below are some of the observable behaviors that concern teachers:

- Fidgets with hands or feet, squirms in seat
- Can't stay seated
- Has difficulty waiting turns in group situations
- Often blurts out answers to questions before the questions are completed
- Doesn't listen well—has trouble following directions
- Is easily distracted
- Has difficulty playing quietly
- Often talks excessively—interrupts others
- Often loses things necessary for activities at home or at school
- Engages in activities without thinking of the consequences

It is important to note here that many of these behaviors are also behaviors of giftedness and/or immaturity.

If, however, your child is diagnosed with ADD or ADHD, talk to the doctor and your child's teacher and tell them you are willing to work with them to help your child. Medication is not necessarily the answer. Many things you can do as a parent will help your child and make life less challenging for you.

- Become informed. Read about ADD/ADHD, use the Internet.
- Join a support group for discussions.
- Take parenting classes on behavioral management for child-

ren with ADD or ADHD.

◆ Accept that it is difficult for your child to concentrate.

◆ Try to stop scolding, nagging, and constant reminding.

◆ Encourage physical activity. Your child needs an outlet for his energy.

◆ Make certain that you establish a home routine that is structured, with consistent enforcement.

◆ Be encouraging and supportive.

◆ Explain the disorder to your child so she understands that it is not "something wrong with you."

◆ Focus on your child's strengths.

◆ Encourage involvement in activities in which he can excel.

◆ Foster responsibility with natural and logical consequences, good and bad.

◆ Provide consistency and structure. Routines and rules are helpful for both you and your child.

◆ Minimize distractions. Provide a quiet, uncluttered place for the child to study or to be alone.

Help your child compensate. Written assignments are usually the most difficult. A computer can be helpful. Written reminders in notebooks, on the wall, etc. can be helpful without the verbal nagging.

ॐ ॐ ॐ

Learning disabilities/struggling learners

Children who have learning disabilities have special needs in education. They also have special needs from their parents. Such children are often of average or above average in intelligence, even gifted, but have discrepancies between what they should be able to achieve and what they are actually achieving in some areas. Often these disabilities are not diagnosed until at least the upper elementary grades when it becomes quite pronounced and the child is referred for testing.

PL94-142 (The Education for All Handicapped Children Act) defines children with learning disabilities as: "Those children who have a disorder in one or more of the basic psychological processes involved in understanding or using language, spoken or written, which disorder may manifest itself in imperfect ability to listen, think, speak, read, write, spell, or do mathematical calculations."

The Act goes on to say: "A team may determine that a child has a specific learning disability if (1) the child does not achieve commensurate with his/her age and ability levels in one or more areas...when provided with learning experiences appropriate for the child's age and ability levels, and (2) the team finds that the child has a discrepancy between achievement and intellectual ability in one or more of these areas."

ठ‍ठ ठ‍ठ ठ‍ठ

Until the child has been referred and a discrepancy recognized, parents often believe their child is not achieving because the child isn't trying hard enough. Homework becomes a dreaded time in the household because the child is overwhelmed by the amount or the kind of work required. If the disability is one of auditory memory, he may not be able to remember the teacher's directions for completing the homework. Such cases may involve auditory processing or an inability to screen out extraneous noise. As a result, the classroom becomes chaotic for the child, who simply can't concentrate. What can a parent do?

First, observe and listen. If you see a discrepancy in one or more areas, talk to your child's teacher. The teacher may or may not agree with you, but she will now be alerted to what may be a problem with your child's learning, and will begin to take notes. The teacher may ask the school psychologist to observe or confer with last year's teacher. In most school districts, the next step is a student study team meeting involving you, the teacher, the psychologist, the resource specialist, and sometimes the principal. The team will note your child's strengths and weaknesses and may refer your child for testing to determine if indeed there is a significant discrepancy. The knowledge gained from the testing will be invaluable to you and the teacher in working through your child's strengths and adjusting for weaknesses.

As a parent, it is important to help your child understand what those strengths and weaknesses are. You can also share with your child that you, too, find some tasks difficult, and that everyone has similar problems in some areas. Explain the results of the testing to your child. Explain what a learning disability is, and how it is an obstacle to learning. Once your child understands that there is a reason for her difficulty, she will probably be relieved, and will learn to compensate for the difficulty. Assure your child that having difficulty does not mean she is mentally retarded. The Resource Specialist can show you and the classroom teacher ways to work with your child. Often he can provide you with games and ideas to help your child at home—simple things like making eye contact before giving directions, giving one direction at a time, playing memory games, etc.

You can also help your child feel protected from being teased or bullied about the learning disability. Spend some time talking about fears. Acknowledge his feelings, and don't downplay the significance of those feelings. Talk about what might happen, and help him plan for what he could say or do if teasing occurs (from smiling or walking away to acknowledging, "Yeah, it's hard for me," or "Yes, I'm better at other things"). Perhaps the person teasing could even be engaged in conversation and asked what things are easy or what's difficult for him.

ৰু ৩৫ ৩৫ ৰু

There are excellent biographies in the library about famous and successful men and women who had to cope with learning disabilities like dyslexia and were often considered dull or dim-witted by their families and teachers. We laugh at the evaluation of people like Albert Einstein, Tom Cruise, Whoopi Goldberg, and Winston Churchill. Reading about their failures, struggles, and successes may help your child deal with his own difficulties.

The important thing for you to remember is to focus on your child's strengths. Children with learning disabilities begin to feel "dumb" or inadequate because learning in some areas is so difficult. When your child voices those thoughts you can counter with, "I know that's a problem for you, and I know you are work-ing on ways to make it easier. Your teacher and I want to help, too. You are so good at the computer, let's see if you can work on your writing assignment there (or help your brother with math or whatever will provide a taste of success)." Success really does breed success. Create opportunities that foster competence in ar-eas of strength as well as opportunities for responsibility. Encour-age your child to focus on specific goals and skills she wishes to develop so she can feel good about her growth in those areas. Your child needs to have successful experiences to have a feeling of competence and self-esteem.

*"I considered home schooling, but then
I realized they'd be home all day."*

Troubled youth

Children who have experienced trauma in their lives at one time or another frequently act out in ways that are difficult to deal with. This is common among those who have experienced divorce or separation of parents, a death in the family, the loss of a parent or sibling, a new step-parent, threatening illness or personal abuse. For some children, this sort of trauma can result in eating disorders or self-destructive behaviors. For others, it may be manifested through violence to others, temper tantrums, disobedience, or social withdrawal. Such behavior can usually be attributed to the inability of the child to deal with the inner stress that he feels. Some young people find that drinking alcohol or using drugs helps to relieve the stress, hurt and anxiety they feel. Others are inclined to look for peers with similar problems and to submit to peer pressure for sex, reckless behavior, stealing, truancy, or rebellion against authority.

While the immediate response of many parents is to take punitive measures to deal with the behavior, this seldom corrects the real problem. Instead, parents need to address the underlying reason for the behavior. This may necessitate consulting with a counselor or child psychologist. The important thing is to be realistic about what is happening, rather than engaging in denial and wishful thinking, hoping that the problem will take care of itself or that the child will outgrow it. Take immediate steps to understand the problem and work with the child to address the problem rather than just the symptom. In many cases, the problem may have been caused by actions taken in the past that cannot be changed. In such situations, the child may need counseling to help resolve the conflict and deal with it in more acceptable ways.

ॐ ॐ ॐ

Dealing with troubled youth makes being a parent extremely difficult. It is natural to love your child, even when he or she is acting like a monster. This makes it difficult to take the actions that are in the child's best interests. But this is the responsibility of a parent, even if it costs you the temporary friendship of your child. There are numerous agencies and resources for help and guidance, including the school, the church, social services, child protective services, juvenile authorities, as well as private agencies. Your primary motivation for seeking help is to realize that the problem is apt to get worse and result in serious trouble unless you take the initiative to address it now. So seek whatever help you need to perhaps save your child's life and chance of success as an adult.

ॐ ॐ ॐ

Physical disabilities

Some of the most successful, self-esteeming children we know are those who have physical handicaps. In talking to their parents, we find a commonality in their parenting. Whether it is spina bifida, Down syndrome, epilepsy, or Tourette's syndrome, these children have been encouraged to take on as much responsibility as possible. Parental expectations have been high with a no-nonsense approach to accomplishment. Friends, family, and teachers are sometimes asked to treat the children as if they were not handicapped, though some accommodations usually have to be made.

ॐ ॐ ॐ

Today, more and more physically handicapped children are participating in regular classrooms. One child with spina bifida went through elementary school with assistance from a paraprofessional who volunteered bathroom attendance when needed, and the bus driver who had a seat reserved for her at the front of the bus. Classmates sometimes carried her books. Her teachers excused her tardiness in the morning because it took her a long time to walk from the bus to the classroom. She took pride, however, in doing as much for herself as possible. Children with Down syndrome, epilepsy and those with Tourette's have also been accommodated in regular classrooms.

In each case, it was necessary to gain school cooperation and understanding. Parents went to school and talked with educators and classmates about the disability, how the child wanted to be treated, and what might happen because of the disability. It was a remarkable and enlightening experience for all concerned.

Parents have confided to us that at first the news of their child's physical disability was devastating. Children are supposed to be one of God's miracles. They are supposed to be perfect. Our children are sometimes considered extensions of ourselves, products of a union of love between man and wife. Some parents simply feel inadequate to care for a child with these special needs. Some parents take on too much responsibility for the child because they pity the child and want to compensate through love and attention. Some parents even feel guilty or believe that the disability, especially if it is hereditary, is their fault! In some cases, care for the disabled child creates neglect of siblings and spouse— some unions cannot withstand the demands of such care. Siblings sometimes resent the "special" child who takes up so much of their parents' love and attention.

ॐ ॐ ॐ

In households that are successfully navigating the parenting of children with disabilities, the home environment is warm, loving, and secure. Expectations are high. Parents are careful not to be over-protective or to create the impression that the child is helpless and unable to deal with life without help. All family members share responsibilities and family time. Family meetings are common. When problems are discussed, parents ask, "What do you plan to do?" or "How might we deal with this problem?" They talk about possible obstacles like attitude and inability to do all the things their peers can do like skipping rope and then all the things they can do and do well. When Marilyn had polio as a child, there was a period of time when she could not walk. It was then that she developed her great love for reading and an understanding of the other things that are important in life. A child who cannot skip may become a great musician because he has the time and will to practice and persevere. He might also become expert at board games like checkers or chess.

Parents can help children with disabilities anticipate what might happen. They can prepare their children for situations like teasing, dealing with physical obstacles, or seizures when they are at school. What could the child do? What can others do in such situations? Children should feel comfortable in expressing their fears and feelings, but should also be encouraged to turn negative feeling into positive thoughts and actions. We inherit many things from our parents, including our physical constitution and our innate abilities. Sometimes, children inherit a disability. What is most significant, however, is how children respond to these inherited factors. Where one child may view some physical characteristic as a "handicap," another may see it as strength.

Again, opportunities for all family members to contribute to the well-being of others helps the child look beyond himself and creates a positive attitude about his own disability. Once again, biographies are beneficial, as children are able to read about others who, especially as young people, were able to overcome disabilities and become highly successful and productive human beings.

ॐ ॐ ॐ

Bob played tennis with a friend, Roger Crawford, who was physically handicapped. When Roger Crawford was born, he had just a thumb-like projection coming directly out of his right forearm and a thumb and one finger sticking out of his left forearm. He had no palms and had only three toes on one shrunken foot. The doctor said Roger would probably never walk or care for himself, but his parents refused to accept this. He had to hold a pencil with both arms to write, but his parents encouraged him to learn to do this. They also encouraged him to participate in sports. He managed to play on the football team in high school, and in college became a tennis player who won 22 matches against just 11 losses. He became the first physically handicapped tennis player to achieve certification as a teaching professional. Roger now speaks throughout the country with the message, "The only difference between you and me is that you can see my handicap, and you may try to hide yours, for we all have handicaps."

Children with disabilities need to know that you have faith in them and that you trust them to be all they can be. Fulfill your agreements and deal with your child in a calm, predictable, and consistent fashion. Encourage self-responsibility, decision-making and problem-solving on their own, and use the language of encouragement to support their efforts. Most important of all, let them know that your love is unconditional, a foundation to give them both roots and wings.

ॐ ॐ ॐ

Autism

The number of children diagnosed with autism and its closely related disorder, Asperger's syndrome, is exploding in the United States. A few years ago, it was estimated that only 1 in 2,000 children suffered from these problems, but today it is estimated that 1 in 500 are affected. Autism is a neurological disorder believed to stunt the part of the brain that controls social interaction and communication. According to the Autism Society of American, more than a million people in this country suffer from one of the autistic disorders. It is now believed that autism "runs" in families; consequently, parents sometimes feel a special guilt. Children with autism have many of the same special needs as children with physical or learning disabilities, but they also have special needs of their own.

ॐ ॐ ॐ

Children with autism seem to reside in a special world of their own, making it difficult for them to communicate and form relationships with others. About 10% are relatively high functioning, while others are mentally retarded or have serious language delays. Some may excel at something in detail, such as spelling or playing a musical instrument, but become overwhelmed when trying to navigate the world at large or when relating with others. Symptoms usually appear before these children are three years old. Those who are not high functioning are usually socially withdrawn. They may resist attention and affection, seeming indifferent to parents' comings and goings. They lack understanding of cues such as a wink or smile and avoid eye contact.

They can be physically aggressive at times, particularly when they are in a strange environment or are over-stimulated. At times, they may break things, attack others, or harm themselves. Obviously, these are very demanding needs and challenging to parents. Parents of autistic children have confided that the inability to communicate is the most painful and difficult aspect of the disorder. The child faces frustration in making efforts to make his needs known, and the parent faces frustration in meeting the child's needs. Some autistic children display affection by pressing their cheeks against another person's, or by touching; but that display of affection can quickly change to one of aggression or rejection. This can be very painful for a loving parent to endure.

ॐ ॐ ॐ

Most children with autism can be identified early because of their difficulty in making eye contact, looking at faces, or responding to others. About 30% of these children appear to be developing normally until, sometimes overnight, their behavior changes. Others seem to have difficulty relating shortly after birth. Intervening at a young age while a child's brain is developing seems to make a significant difference in the child's ability to relate to the outside world. Unfortunately, it is sometimes difficult for parents to locate resources that can help, but proper training and environment can do much to enable autistic children to function normally. Because you have the best chances for success when treatment is begun early, it is important that you have your child examined for autism if you begin to believe that your child is not responding normally. So, what symptoms should parents look for?

At six months, these are common symptoms of children diagnosed with autism:

- Not making eye contact with parents during interaction
- Not cooing or babbling
- Not smiling when parents smile
- Not participating in vocal turn-taking (baby makes a sound, adult makes a sound, and so forth)
- Not responding to peek-a-boo game

At fourteen months, these might be symptoms to look for:

- ◆ No attempts to speak
- ◆ Not pointing, waving or grasping
- ◆ No response when name is called
- ◆ Indifferent to others
- ◆ Repetitive body motions such as rocking or hand flapping
- ◆ Fixation on a single object
- ◆ Oversensitivity to textures, smells, or sounds
- ◆ Strong resistance to change in routine
- ◆ Any loss of language

While all children may exhibit some of these symptoms on occasion, the autistic child is apt to exhibit these symptoms frequently.

❦ ❦ ❦

These children can learn skills, but it is important to break down into smaller steps the desired skills or social behaviors and reward them for repeating each of these steps. Early educational therapy can train autistic children to learn words, identify faces, and make eye contact—skills other children pick up just by watching and mimicking others that autistic children do not. It is therefore important to train them in proper social behavior and what others normally expect in terms of behavior. If possible, parents should work with a behavioral specialist to help their child learn acceptable ways to express frustrations and feelings. Autistic children often need help in learning how to look at faces, how to listen to voices, and how to interpret various expressions and voice sounds. Using pictures to teach the proper words to identify objects, colors, or numbers can be helpful. Most experts feel that intensive therapy—which usually includes 20 or more hours a week of behavioral, speech, physical, and occupational therapies—can improve a child's functioning.

Most of these children have difficulty in some form of sensory integration. Some children cannot handle loud sounds or hearing several voices at once, so they are likely to cover their ears. Such children respond best when there are no other distracting sounds and directions are whispered to them. Others are distracted by too many visual stimuli. For this reason, parents need to be sensitive to their child's sensitivity and strive to create an environment that reduces the child's exposure to multiple stimuli. Recently, perhaps due to the large numbers of children being diagnosed with autism, more money is being spent on research.

ᐁ ᐁᐁ ᐁ

Asperger's Syndrome

This syndrome is a developmental disorder with many of the same symptoms of autism. It is usually referred to as high functioning autism, because people with this disorder generally display higher mental performance than those with typical autism. Gifted children are sometimes diagnosed with Asperger's syndrome. Like autism, it is a life-long condition. It is characterized by poor motor coordination, obsessing on a narrow interest, inflexibility about routines, and "robotic" speech. Children with this disorder typically lack social skills, have difficulty relating to others, and feel little empathy towards others.

As with other disorders, parents of a child with Asperger's Syndrome need to become knowledgeable about the disorder, and should seek support from individuals and organizations dedicated to advocating for children with this special need. There are many helpful websites for these organizations, including autism-society.org, autism-info.com, or ASPEN (Asperger Syndrome Educational Network). Other parents can also be a great resource for finding the right treatments.

What can you do if you suspect autism or Asperger's? You can begin by getting an evaluation from a developmental pediatrician with expertise in the field of autism. Know your rights! It is every state's mandate to provide a free evaluation and early intervention services. There is no cure for these disorders, but there are treatments that can make a difference, such as speech therapy, occupational therapy, behavioral therapy, educational therapy, and medication. Sometimes special diets or eliminating certain food groups can help. You will need to protect your child from bullying or being picked on by others. Use visual cues, and build on your child's special interests. Avoid escalating power struggles. Encourage your autistic child to take on as much responsibility for himself as possible. Look for strengths and positive attributes in your child. Teach self-care and life skills. Most important, don't neglect yourself— look for support and care for yourself as well as your child. Many states offer funds for respite workers to give parents a break from the constant care required. Reach out for knowledge, assistance, and emotional support in this difficult parenting, and acknowledge when your care is not enough—if needed, there are many people and organizations that can help you find the right place for your special child. And know that you are a very special parent.

Some activities to consider:

1. Some children are greatly calmed by physical pressure. Try dressing your child in a heavy vest or coat.

2. Help your child develop personal skills that don't involve communicating with others. Encourage her to draw, sing, or use a musical instrument.

3. Try to create a structured situation where the young child is encouraged to interact and respond, rather than allowing him to retreat into his own private world.

Children of divorce

Children of divorce have special needs, and so do their parents. Though divorce is fairly common (almost half of all marriages end in divorce), it continues to have a profound effect on children. Young children find it hard to understand and may act out their confusion. They often believe it is their fault that father or mother left. They believe if only they had been better or had better grades the divorce would never have happened. They need help in understanding that they are not bad, so they can let go of the feelings of guilt for their parents breaking up.

Children and parents go through stages of grieving at the loss. Many children think the family has ended—and it has, as they know it, but their relationship may continue as it is. Children need both parents and/or outsiders to help them understand that the family has changed, but that they are still part of a family. It can be helpful to look around and discover that there are many different forms of family. Children learn that they now have two houses and two sets of rules. It is helpful when parents and stepparents can agree on major issues and display a united front in making major decisions. Children are often confused as to where they are supposed to be. Issues like leaving homework or personal items behind at one parent's house are serious matters to children. You need to help your children deal with such issues in a calm, matter-of-fact manner. Having two sets of many items, one for each house, and having a calendar with days circled as to where they should be, is helpful. Schools are accustomed to providing two sets of report cards when it is requested. Taking away stress by providing structure is very important to your children's well-being, and will help them accept the divorce. It is vital for the child to know the expectations of each parent. As a parent, you can add to your child's sense of security by having a plan that anticipates possible difficulties.

ॐ ॐ ॐ

When someone in a family dies, there is a ceremony and a period of grieving, and friends and family gather in support and care; but in a divorce, especially one that is acrimonious, friends and family may stay away or side with one parent or the other. Parents become preoccupied with the issues of divorce and their own grief and perhaps a new partner just when children need their attention the most. Children have probably been feeling the stress long before it came to divorce, and their stress will last long after the papers are signed. They see that it might happen, and they worry. The people they love are saying unkind things to each other. Children may reflect that modeling by lashing out at someone else to ease their own hurt. Children can also become manipulative by saying what each parent wants to hear or "playing" one against the other.

Children go through their stages of grief, beginning with denial. "This is really not happening," or "They might get back together again." The next stage is usually struggling with emotions, feeling confused, overwhelmed, and rejected. At this time, children need to be able to express their feelings. Outsiders or new stepparents can often play the role of impartial listener, validating the children's feelings and acknowledging that it's okay to feel the way they do.

ॐ ॐ ॐ

It may take years, but if all goes well, children will finally go through a reorganization and acceptance of "what is and shall be." Everyone concerned must keep in mind that children are very vulnerable and may go through the stages again and again. Children need a foundation of physical and emotional security that you, as their parent, can provide through consistency, structure, and unfailing caring. You can talk about marriage, and why people marry, and how people change and make mistakes. The most important thing for children to know is they are not a mistake and that a divorce doesn't mean parents stop loving or taking care of their children.

Divorce means single parenting whether there is full custody or shared, and you as the parent will have your own stages of grief and special needs. When we have talked with people about the problems and pitfalls of single parenting, the custodial parent usually tells us that the number one issue is lack of time. Working full-time, shopping, cooking, cleaning, helping with homework without a partner can be overwhelming. It can also cause resentment of the non-custodial parent, who may be envisioned as being free as a bird until the children visit, when it's a holiday for all concerned. The custodial parent has an awesome responsibility, and unless there is emotional support and time off, it can be defeating. Many single parents are exhausted, worried about finances, and have no one to "spell them." Children can also become manipulative by saying what each parent wants to hear or "playing" one against the other. Single parents also have no one to join in decision-making or assuming responsibility on a daily basis. Some parents who are lonely make the mistake of treating the child as their confidante and their friend, establishing a mutually dependent relationship, which is usually not in the child's best interest. Others become neglectful of the child's needs because of their own needs.

Single parents also say that there is a need for an adult of the opposite sex to be a model and mentor for their child, especially if the other parent, father or mother, is very part-time. One mother asked, "How do I teach my son the boy basics? I try to play catch with him but I don't know how to teach him manliness, and how do I talk to him about puberty and dating?" In such cases, grandparents and adult friends can be invaluable in taking on these roles. They can become models and mentors, listening and showing understanding as special buddies. They can teach new skills, as well as praise, encourage, and reassure.

They can also do the same for you as a parent. Chances are you need some of the same things your child does, so don't be afraid to reach out for friendship and help to take care of the caregiver. You really can't give what you don't have; so take care of yourself and model good social and emotional well-being for your child of divorce.

ᘒ ᘒ ᘒ

Stepfamilies

Today, one in four children experiences the separation or divorce of parents, and millions learn to adjust to a new family situation. A stepfamily or a re-ordered family is formed when a parent takes a new partner or when parents take on the responsibility for a foster child or the child of other parents. Children who become part of this new family typically undergo periods of great stress due to the many problems they may be experiencing.

Some are feeling the loss of a parent, friends, and the familiarity of their former home. Others are recovering from the problems of previous parental relationships. Many children suffer from insecurity regarding the long-term nature of this new relationship, as well as changes in parental expectations and enforcement procedures. In many cases, the children may suffer from divided loyalty, anxieties about favoritism, feelings of rejection, and differences in parenting style between the parents. All of these problems require that parents create a loving, caring environment with clear, fair, and consistent standards.

The marriage of a new couple can cause problems in itself. There are apt to be jealousies, resentments of new demands and expectations that need to be dealt with. For children of divorce, it may finally confirm that their original family cannot be recreated. Parents obviously need to devote time to resolving issues related to different attitudes towards child-rearing and standards of behavior. Parents also need time to develop a relationship with stepchildren and to be alone with their own children to reassure them that their love for them has not changed.

༖ ༖ ༖

Being a stepparent is thus a challenge. Sometimes partners think that because they love each other so much, problems will be easy to deal with. However, the emotional problems the children experience need to be addressed with more than just love. There has to be a real commitment from both adults to make the new family work—for the children and for the adults. Stepparents have a difficult role which is compounded when they bring children of their own into the new union. "Blended families" can work. We may remember the television family "The Brady Bunch," but in that situation there were no ex-spouses or apparent financial worries, nor are we all as patient and wise as Mr. and Mrs. Brady.

There will be many pitfalls for the stepfamily, but the best problem-stopper is the unity and love of the marital union. Ideally, children have come to know and appreciate the "new" parent before the marriage takes place. Unfortunately, sometimes during the dating days of divorce, children are introduced to multiple adults who could be their new mother or father, and they become fearful of attachment to someone who may only be temporary. Modeling a loving relationship is the best thing you can do for children. At first the "newcomer" may be viewed as a competitor for mother or father's love, and may be greeted with resentment and suspicion. So it is especially important that children understand there will be no abandonment, that this is a permanent situation, and that love given is not limited to the partner but includes all members of the family. Liking and loving the "new" parent will not take love away from the biological parent. Getting to know one another, especially with one-on-one time, builds relationships.

ॐ ॐ ॐ

Stepfamilies may always have sibling rivalry, but there is also sibling love and concern for one another as members of a family. Rivalry between step-siblings is fairly common, and can cause irreparable harm if it becomes, "YOUR CHILD!" and "MY CHILD!" Being fair and equitable in all things is even more important to step-children. If one adult in the new marriage has a different philosophy of parenting and discipline than the other, the differences need to be resolved—again, ideally, before the marriage takes place. Like all parenting, parenting a stepfamily must include an agreed-on philosophy of discipline and continual communication between partners, so children do not receive mixed messages or succeed in manipulating one parent against another. If children are included in family activities, blended traditions, and decision-making, with patience and love, they will establish the feelings of security and belonging that are so essential to their development and to the well-being of the union and family.

When these problems are recognized and efforts made to address them, stepfamilies can have positive rewards. Through the stepfamily, children gain a wider family; and working together to solve difficulties can be a valuable learning experience for children. Children of stepfamilies often come through into adult life with a greater capacity to adapt. They can learn to be more tolerant and to compromise, and can be enriched by experiencing and learning about different lifestyles first hand. Stepfamilies can also bring a sense of belonging and comfort to children who have not experienced that before.

Summary

Every child is unique, so a key to effective parenting is being able to adapt to these unique differences. Boys and girls need to be treated differently, but without enforcing stereotype behaviors on them. The key is to help them feel comfortable in being who they are. As they face social problems with their peers help them explore different options about how to deal with their problem and let them choose what they feel most comfortable in doing rather than prescribing what they should do. When children are faced with separation or divorce in the family, it is important for them to realize that they were not the cause of the problem. Step-parents have unique problems in raising step-children, but these problems can be minimized when both parents can reach agreement regarding expectations, standards, and discipline.

Chapter 9
Meeting the Needs
of Gifted Children

৵ৼ ৵ৼৼ ৵ৼ

Myths and misconceptions about gifted children have diminished the perceived need for special attention, but ask any parent who has a gifted child and you will quickly learn that these children do, indeed, have special needs.

When a child starts arranging the alphabet cereal in sequential order or begins to create words with the individual pieces, you might begin to suspect a high level of intelligence. When a two-year-old who has been introduced to the Spanish language on Sesame Street stands up in the crib and repeats all the Spanish phrases correctly, or when your teenager prefers a history magazine to *Seventeen*, you know you have a "different" child. One parent said she knew her child was gifted at the age of four years when she, on leaving the church service, tugged at the minister's tunic and asked, "Do you think God and Zeus get along?" One parent told us how her one-year-old put a cloth book in her mouth and crawled over to her so she could have it read to her, and has been reading voraciously ever since!

Some parents have said they knew their children were different but thought perhaps it was a bad thing. They didn't seem interested in the same things as their peers, and were constantly questioning. Sometimes the gifted child would pursue one topic for months to the exclusion of everything else. One parent knew her child was highly intelligent, but didn't realize how intelligent she was until the mother was studying for the law exam and her daughter, who was then a teenager, took the practice exam and passed it with flying colors! The same daughter believed she could eliminate high school and go straight to college, but she voiced the acceptance of the importance of high school for her social development!

ॐ ॐ ॐ

Characteristics of gifted children

Gifted children are challenging for parents and teachers. Joan Smutny is an expert on the young gifted. Some of the behaviors she finds common in five- and six-year-olds:

- ◆ express curiosity about many things
- ◆ ask thoughtful questions
- ◆ have extensive vocabularies and use complex sentence structures
- ◆ solve problems in unique ways
- ◆ have good memories
- ◆ exhibit original imaginations
- ◆ are fast learners and exhibit wit and humor
- ◆ are very observant
- ◆ have sustained attention span in things of interest
- ◆ are interested in reading

A compilation of other characteristics attributed to the gifted includes:

- ◆ divergent thinking ability
- ◆ excitability
- ◆ perceptiveness
- ◆ passionate interest
- ◆ perfectionism
- ◆ abstract thinking
- ◆ advanced sense of justice and fairness
- ◆ awareness of global issues
- ◆ preferring the company of intellectual peers
- ◆ perceiving subtle cause and effect relationships
- ◆ having many hobbies, interests, and collections
- ◆ intensity

Obviously, not all gifted children have all of these characteristics, but if you see many of these behaviors and attributes exhibited on a consistent basis, your child is probably intellectually gifted.

"My teacher said I could keep it all summer!"

Provide opportunities to grow intellectually

Many children fail to achieve at the level one might expect. This is often the case even when a child is intellectually gifted. This happens for a variety of reasons. Some grow up in an impoverished home environment without the stimulation of magazines, books to read, or intellectually stimulating games or toys. Others grow up in situations that are filled with stress and conflict or where they are abused. Research has shown that children brought up in such conditions often fail to achieve their full potential. Those who feel rejected and unloved can score as much as 30 points lower on intelligence tests. On the other hand, when children are brought up in an environment where they have an opportunity to explore different materials, engage in stimulating conversations, play games that require creative thinking, and experience frequent opportunities to learn new things, they can significantly increase their measured intelligence.

It is therefore important that parents search for ways to expand children's creative and thinking abilities. Strive to give life to your gifted child's ideas with the language of encouragement rather than generalized praise. Research indicates that praising children for their intelligence saps their motivation and they are likely to overstate their scores to their peers. Praise your child for effort and persevering when he or she struggles to accomplish a challenging task. Encourage risk-taking and asking for help. Make your home environment a safe place for your child to make mistakes and try out new roles. Remind the child that mistakes are opportunities for learning. Be very clear and realistic about your expectations. Gifted children are their own severest critics, with a tendency toward perfectionism.

Some activities to consider:

1. Perform mental gymnastics with your gifted child: chess, checkers, crossword puzzles, Scrabble, cryptograms, word jumbles, mathematical puzzles.

2. Have your child pick an object and then try to sell it back to you to use in a manner for which it was not intended.

3. Offer your child stimulating toys that encourage creativity.

ॐ ॐ ॐ

Special needs of gifted children

Gifted children are challenging. The nature of giftedness creates special needs in children that often create conflicts from interaction with the environment in which they function.

Most gifted children are essentially introverts, and their super sensitivity creates a vulnerability that sometimes calls for protection and comfort. Help your child understand the nature of his giftedness. One of the biggest problems for a gifted child under age ten is his lack of understanding of what being gifted means.

It's a secret! He knows he is different but is not sure why or whether it's bad or a good thing to be. If your child has been identified as gifted in school, go over the test results with him, especially indicators of weaknesses and strengths. Rarely are children gifted across the board, and it's important for them to understand that, because that is one of the myths of giftedness and sometimes one of the expectations. The author, Judy Gailbraith, tells us that it is also one of the gripes of the gifted. In a democratic, egalitarian society we are still having difficulty with the idea of superior intelligence, because the implication is that the rest of us are somehow inferior.

Probably one of the most important things you can do for your child's social and emotional development is listen! Listening builds trust and is a lifeline for your child between the inner self and the outside world. Validate his intelligence by listening in a serious and accepting manner to fears, concerns, and ideas. Prize him as a learner. Help your child identify his feelings and affirm them as real.

Structure is important to gifted children, as is having choice within that structure. They need to understand cause and effect and the nature of consequences. Develop shared control by defining limits and choices and the consequences of each. Help them anticipate and plan for the "what ifs." Give them plenty of lead-time before asking them to complete something or to change to another activity. Give them explanations for what you want them to do and why you want them to do it.

$$\mathcal{L} \mathcal{L} \mathcal{L}$$

Help them understand themselves

Gifted children need to know how they are similar and different from others. It is important to raise the perception and narrow the difference between how they perceive themselves and how they perceive the expectations of others. Often, gifted children do not develop equally in all areas. They may feel different and inferior to their chronological peers who have better dexterity or more advanced social sophistication. They do not understand the interests of their peers and find little in common with many of them. It is important they receive validation of the worth of their giftedness from you, their parents, and from others whose opinion they value.

We must help our gifted children find their own identity through building self-awareness and a realistic self-concept. This includes helping them accept their physical image and strengths and weaknesses. Children develop a positive self-image by taking pride in who they are. Help them distinguish between what they can and cannot do. Promote pride—not guilt or anxiety—in their intellectual ability and encourage them to acknowledge their talents and strengths. Gifted children need acceptance and approval as individuals, particularly if all of their self-worth is linked to accomplishments, performances, or products.

$$\mathcal{S}\!\!\!\!\!\sim \;\; \mathcal{S}\!\!\!\!\!\sim \;\; \mathcal{S}\!\!\!\!\!\sim$$

A serious dilemma in self-esteem arises when children feel they are valued only because they are smart, get good grades, or perform well, while other children are valued for just being alive! Gifted children sometimes wonder if they will be loved and valued if they stop achieving. The compliant gifted child who spends an entire childhood pleasing her parents and teachers with grades or performances may find little pleasure in accomplishments as an adult. Gifted children sometimes perceive their accomplishments as not as good as those of siblings, or they believe they can't meet parental expectations. They may see themselves as unacceptable, and may need help in discovering good things about themselves and in seeing themselves in positive ways. Appreciate them as valued human beings, not because they get good grades or perform well.

Many gifted children also suffer from excessive self-criticism and the tendency to be a perfectionist in their early years. Learning may come easy for them, but they may set unrealistic expectations for themselves. They may need guidance from parents to avoid setting excessively high expectations that cause them stress and frustration later on. They need to understand that it's okay to make mistakes and that it's okay to ask for help. Encourage them to read biographies of people who fail and learn from failure like Thomas Edison and Henry Ford.

It is also important for gifted children to understand why they are here. Help them determine how they best fit in this world. One young, gifted learner expressed frustration this way: "You know the world is full of idiots!" Gifted children do not suffer fools gladly. They believe that the world is in the hands of incompetent adults who are accepting of injustice and incongruity. They often come across as bossy or argumentative, and become so frustrated they want to drop out—and sometimes do. They can also become silent and simply wait for others to catch up. It is important for parents to help gifted children value and accept those who are less able. It is also important to teach them socially acceptable and respectful ways to voice their concerns and express their ideas. Help them disagree without being disagreeable. Social skills do not seem to come easily to gifted students, and they need parental help in understanding their feelings and being able to express them in socially acceptable ways. Sometimes, the solution is to encourage them to develop leadership skills so they can direct others rather than be frustrated by the inept efforts of others.

$$\sim \sim \sim$$

It is also important to help gifted children expand their interests for their own social and emotional development and to find common ground with others. Gifted children often have trouble connecting with others, leading to a sense of social isolation. They don't want the stigma of being different, especially as they approach adolescence. Research shows that it is important for gifted children to spend some time with their intellectual peers, to stimulate their thinking and for their sense of identity and belonging, as they realize they are not out there alone. There are other children like them who understand them. Gifted children need to make connections with others and to have empathy for the feelings of others. Role-playing and taking on another point of view helps them expand their perceptions and appreciate the ideas of others. Parents can help their children with people skills by modeling, by inviting children over and talking about ways to make conversation, and to be host or hostess, etc.

ତେ ତିତି ତେ

One of the best ways to help gifted children feel that they are a part of a larger community is by encouraging them to be of service to others. Model and mentor your child in your conversations and in your actions. Talk about how it must feel to need help and to receive it. Get the family together to collect and distribute food for the homeless or work in a soup kitchen. Point out how Grandma can use help trimming her bushes or how much she would appreciate a visit from her grandchild. Helping the gifted child to assume responsibilities in the family also helps the child feel connected, and teaches the child about being accountable for one's behaviors and actions. Do not allow your gifted child to exhibit socially inappropriate behavior. Do not tolerate the child humiliating or putting down other people or children. Build and teach social skills. Insist on mutual respect. Talk to your child about when it's important to be unique and when it's important to be part of a group. Explain that each member of the family contributes to the strength of the family. Some people are intellectual stretchers, while others are risk takers, or chicken soup people who care for others, or cheerleaders.

ତେ ତିତି ତେ

Some activities to consider:

1. Make it easy for your child to share her feelings and frustrations with you. Keep the lines of communication open as long as possible.

2. Set up activities or adventures for your child. Encourage him to bring one or two friends to come along.

Help them focus their energy

From pre-school on, many gifted children tend to be unusually focused in their expenditure of time and energy with great will power and perseverance for getting what they want. They are able to set their own goals in areas of their interests. They often need help, however, in understanding the relevance of doing something that is outside their zone of competence or interest. They also often have problems with time management and organization. Because learning is so easy for them, they often do not establish good work habits and may not value effort. Having many talents and interests can be a problem. They see so many possibilities and situations that their time and energy can be fragmented. Therefore they need help to establish realistic goals, to determine resources, and to set benchmarks along the way to meet their goals.

ॐ ॐ ॐ

It's also important to teach your gifted child planning skills. Because gifted students often wait until the last minute to write a paper; the paper will not be their best effort, but they are often praised for it nonetheless. As a result, they never reach the limits of their capacity. You can counteract this by insisting on work that is challenging for them and by establishing an expectation of quality and accountability. Find ways for them to go into greater depth and complexity in areas of interest. As long as they don't push themselves, they will never achieve at their full potential. Encourage risk-taking and the willingness to fail, as well as a work ethic and the responsibility to sustain their motivation. Gifted children are non-conformist by nature, which often comes into conflict with the conformity required by our schools and society. To help them thrive in the world, gifted children need help building classroom survival skills like listening, asking for help, bringing materials to class, completing assignments and turning them in at the appropriate time and place, and contributing to classroom discussions.

Introduce your gifted children to new experiences and interests, but hold them accountable to try these experiences for a suitable length of time, perhaps determined jointly by you and your child. Otherwise, gifted children may flit from one interest to another without any real involvement or accountability. Help them determine their needs and interests.

Often gifted children develop a strong passion in a particular area of interest. Even though we as parents want our children to be "well rounded," this is sometimes not possible for gifted children. Support self-initiated activities, and speak the language of encouragement. Share your passion and encourage theirs. Facilitate in-depth pursuit and study in their areas of interest. Their current passion may be a lifelong interest that can become a career, or certainly something they can enjoy for the rest of their lives. Help them set personal goals and ways to achieve them. Remember, gifted children feel strongly about world issues and injustices. Help them take some control over their lives by becoming social activists. They can write letters to the editor or serve on committees or take leadership in trying to right the wrongs they find in this world.

Learning how to use resources effectively is also important to their improved effectiveness. Technology usually comes easy to gifted students and enables them to pursue their interest in great depth and breadth. Problem-solving and decision-making skills are not as easy for them. As we noted earlier, having multiple talents can create a problem. Gifted children can see so many possibilities and nuances. The decision-making process and problem-solving process may have to be reviewed with them often. Gifted children may require help in the determination and analysis of the problem or decision to be made, the listing of possible solutions/decisions, the impact of implementing those decisions/ solutions, and then selecting the best decision or solution for this situation at this time.

Attaining goals, producing quality work, making friendships, pursuing passions, demonstrating caring compassion, and attaining self-knowledge are all cause for celebration and parent joy. Remember to celebrate! Finally, parents of gifted children can model self-care and a healthy life style. Offer hope for the future and believe in their vision for tomorrow, while celebrating who they are today. Enjoy your gifted child!!

Some activities to consider:

1. From time to time, tell your child about unique occupations related to things he is studying in school that might be suitable for him to explore.

2. Have your child make up and tell a story about some topic. In the story the child should include each member of the family, including the family pets.

3. Cut off the words under cartoons and have your child come up with the words she believes would be good words for the cartoon.

ॐ ॐ ॐ

Summary

Having a gifted child can be a mixed blessing. There are times when gifted children can be a source of joy and surprise, but they can also be trying with their endless questions of "why?" There is no question that they often require special attention, especially as they approach adolescence and wish to be just like everyone else rather than the mentally gifted person they are. Of critical importance is helping gifted children to fully explore and understand their unique strengths and abilities and how to capitalize on those qualities. Broaden their interests by exposing them to as many different kinds of experiences as possible and then help them focus on their future. Work with your children to help them profit from their experiences to develop their own sense of wisdom and good judgment. Help them recognize the gifts in others and, most important, encourage effort in using their giftedness to reach their potential and become contributing members of society.

Chapter 10
Foster Parenting

જી જી જી

Parenting "other people's children," as it has been called, has its own special challenges, rules, and rewards. It requires a special kind of parenting. Earlier chapters focused on five essential elements that build the attributes parents want for their children: security, identity, belonging, purpose, and competency. These words take on an entirely different meaning for foster children and foster parents. Although the ideas and suggestions are still relevant and helpful, we must examine the differences for foster parents.

Need for security

Feelings of security, as we said earlier, "come from knowing what to expect, feeling safe and protected, being able to trust others, and having the ability to anticipate what is likely to happen in situations." When children are taken from their homes and family, as bad as that family may be, most want to return to their parent or parents. Children who become wards of the court and move from shelter to foster home to another foster home have no sense of security! Discipline has often been lacking or abusive. Foster children cannot anticipate what will happen next because they are never certain of what lies ahead. "If they don't like me, will they send me away, too? How long will I be here? I can't afford to care about this person. He or she may not be with me tomorrow." These are the words and worries of foster children. Often they will test the foster parents by doing outrageous things to see if their words of affection and love are true. Foster parents need to remember: the hardest children to love are the children who need it the most.

ॐ ॐ ॐ

Security is the foundation for all that follows. It is the first basic need. How can foster parents provide security? First, foster parents must be totally honest and straightforward as to what they can and cannot do, and, yes, indeed, foster parenting is intended to be temporary. The court decides how long the child will be in this family. Foster parents must also be clear about their expectations for behavior, and they must talk about what is important to them, so the child has guidelines for life with the foster family. Rules should be discussed and the consequences, good and bad, that accompany the rules. Too many changes have taken place for most foster children. Routine and structure are paramount in establishing a sense of security. "Bedtime is at nine o'clock. Dinner is at six. We always brush our teeth, take a shower before bed; we can read for forty-five minutes before lights out, etc." All these routines provide structure and security. The foster parent must keep his word and ask the child to do the same. Chores and responsibilities in the family also add to the feeling of being valued and trusted.

ॐ ॐ ॐ

Fears live with the foster child: fear of abandonment, fear of the dark, fear of being alone, fear of being rejected, fear of loving and/or being loved. Fears need to be discussed, and children need to talk about the worst things that can happen to them and then brainstorm what they can do about it. Modeling and mentoring in a consistent manner provides the greatest security for the foster child. Foster parents are providing an alternative environment to the destructive home environments some children come from. Even if the situation is temporary, the foster child will have experienced what life can be like. Foster parents can assure children, "When you are with us you belong with us and we will do anything and everything we can for you." If given enough love and time, foster children will begin to develop a sense of security, a foundation that will stand them in good stead in whatever comes their way in the future.

Foster the sense of identity

Since a child's sense of identity begins with feedback from adults around her, the foster child may arrive with a negative sense of identity and/or a lack of understanding of who she is and how she fits into the world. She may have had no feedback, or may have received mixed messages, so is unsure or confused about the perception of others. Feedback can come from multiple sources. As the child matures, he may feel that everything that has happened is his fault. He is not smart enough or good enough. If only he were better behaved or more attractive or could make things better, life would be different. The foster parent has the huge task of helping the child understand what has happened and why, to begin change and develop a positive self-image. We know that children who grow up with a negative sense of identity can change it to a more positive identity if even one person recognizes their positive qualities and believes in them. The foster parent can do that. The foster parent can help a child figure out who she is and therefore who she can be. Sometimes it is like untangling a badly tangled skein of yarn. Strand by strand, foster parents must learn what kind of feedback the child has had, how the foster child perceives himself, and then determine the child's skills, strengths, shortcomings, and interests. Foster parents can provide positive feedback and opportunities to define and polish those strengths so the yarn is free and each strand ready to be part of a beautiful whole.

ॐ ॐ ॐ

Foster children need to understand their feelings, accept them and be able to express them in appropriate ways. As we noted earlier, children act in ways that are consistent with how they view themselves. Foster children need to discover and value their uniqueness; they need to feel entitled to be respected and loved. No matter how temporary the situation or what lies ahead, this self-understanding and belief will shape and determine their future.

Build feelings of belonging

The sense of belonging is woefully absent from most foster children, and for good reason. As we stated earlier, "We naturally seek the acceptance or approval of friends or others and desire to feel that we belong to a group that accepts us." Often the foster child has been abandoned, rejected, or at best treated as a necessary encumbrance. More often than not, the child is loved, but neglected because of the natural parent's need for drugs, money, or adult relationships. The children often move from place to place and relationships for parent and child are in constant flux. There is no sense of permanence or guarantee of continuity. Once the child enters the court system, that lack of permanence is exacerbated, as again he or she is moved, this time from shelter to foster care to another foster care. Foster children seek and need that feeling of belonging even on a temporary basis. Children who join gangs around the age of eleven are looking for that same sense of acceptance and belonging.

ভেও ৡৢ ভেও

What can the foster parent do? First, there are many suggestions in our chapter on belonging that will be helpful. For the foster child, the need for belonging is more intense and immediate, and for the foster parent providing it, more difficult. Establishing family expectations, routines, and responsibilities is of primary importance. The message is, "We are all members of a family and this is what families do and how family members contribute and support one another." Acceptance and approval come next. Many foster children lack experience in the social skills and behave in socially unacceptable ways. Social skills can be taught. Determine which skills your child needs and then prioritize. Model, role-play, use conflict resolution strategies and be patient. Provide safe opportunities to practice and praise success. Point out "nice" things that people do. Recognize similarities among family members and peers. Include the foster child's new friends in family activities. Use family meetings to plan, discuss, and solve problems together. Make sure the foster child's voice is heard and encouraged. Joining a club or team or troop all contribute to a sense of belonging, but monitor each situation and assist in making it a positive learning experience. The last thing a foster child needs is more rejection.

You may be so successful in creating a sense of belonging the foster child may want to learn more about his own extended family. Seek guidance from the social worker and counselor on this. Once again, no matter how short the stay or how difficult the situation, as a foster parent you will have sown the seeds of belonging that may bloom tomorrow.

Some activities to consider:

1. Do neighborly and societal acts of kindness and caring as a family.

2. Read stories about non-traditional families and families that have overcome adversity by working together.

3. Talk about being a family member even when people leave "the nest" and what that might mean in the event the foster child is removed from the home.

Develop purpose and competence

Foster children often have difficulty finding a sense of purpose, because they see no future, no reason for planning or goal setting or working toward a career. They cannot imagine that their life has any significance. Their goal has been one of survival. Helping foster children recognize their strengths and establish their sense of identity is really a pre-requisite for developing a sense of purpose. As a foster parent, you might begin by discussing with your child how a particular strength may be of great value in the future in a certain profession, or you might help him look at ways to strengthen and improve a particular skill. Then you can help your foster child set realistic short-term goals. Locate resources that can help the child reach a particular goal. As we recommended in our earlier chapter on the "Sense of Purpose," you can provide introductory experiences that might become interests in the future. Encourage the child to read biographies about people who had a passion and pursued it, overcoming many obstacles to do so. Talk with your child about the world of tomorrow. Share articles about what social scientists and futurists think will be important tomorrow. Share your interests and passions, dreams and hopes. Finally, communicate your belief in your foster child and your commitment to help him achieve his own goals and dreams.

జ్న్ జ్న్ జ్న్

The sense of purpose and personal competence build on one another. When a foster child establishes a sense of purpose, this sets the stage for developing competencies. Setting goals and meeting those goals provides a feeling of achievement. Successful experiences then become the evidence of competency. The greatest challenge for foster parents may be developing positive and productive attitudes in the foster child. Repeated failure and uncertainty create a mind-set of negativity, cynicism, and discouragement. The child may feel he has no control over his life and no hope for the future, and so applies little or no effort. He has no confidence that life will or can change for the better. If anything good happens, the child may consider it a strange exception.

What can foster parents do to change negative self-messages and a negative self-image to the positive? You can point out your child's good experiences, and help her analyze her bad experiences to determine what she can learn from them. What was good about a particular experience, and why? What could she have done better or differently? And what might have happened then? Make connections between cause and effect, effort and success. Again, share stories with your foster child about people who failed repeatedly but were ultimately successful, like Babe Ruth or Thomas Edison. Write down quotes that encourage perseverance, and post them in the child's room. Celebrate little successes. Use words of encouragement. Share your own life's lessons, and model and teach your children how to deal with frustration, failure, and losing—as well as winning. Be an advocate for your foster child when he finds himself in difficulty with others. Do not rescue, but advocate and support. Foster children need to know you are there for them, and that you believe in their ability to become successful.

$$\partial \quad \partial \quad \partial$$

Actor Ralph Fiennes talked about success in an interview with *Parade* magazine that seems to be relevant here: "I consider people successful because of how they handle their responsibilities to other people, how they approach the future, people who have a full sense of their life and what to do with it. I call people successful not because they have money or their business is doing well, but because as human beings, they have a fully developed sense of being alive and engaged in a lifetime task of collaboration with other human beings ... Success? Don't you know it is all about being able to extend love to people? This is true, not in a big capital sense but in the everyday little by little, task by task, gesture by gesture, word by word."

This is what foster parents model. This is how foster parents can parent with purpose.

To offer more assistance, we called on a friend of ours who is foster parenting a second generation, this time her own grandson, to share her experiences. Her first foster children were two sisters whom she and her husband learned about through their church when she was a young mother with two children of her own. At first, they offered assistance to these sisters, then temporary help, and eventually they became full-time foster parents for the girls. Today, thirty years later, as a widow looking forward to retirement, she is raising her own grandson who, through no fault of his own, became a high-risk child and a ward of the court.

We asked our friend a series of questions, and are sharing her replies below. (Marilyn has also received training as a court-appointed child advocate, and has included her experience and observations when pertinent.)

Why people want to become foster parents

People usually become foster parents for one of these reasons:

◆ an encompassing unconditional love for children
◆ a desire to rescue, shelter, and protect children in need
◆ a response to a need within the extended family
◆ a response to a need in the community
◆ a personal need for fulfillment
◆ a desire to contribute to society

The job of a foster parent is a temporary one. Reunification of the family is the paramount goal, and the foster parent must be prepared to love and let go, supporting reunification in all thoughts, words, and behaviors. In some cases, the reunification process results in a foster child having multiple sets of foster parents, moving every few months.

ଔଔ ଔଔ ଔଔ

As a foster parent, your life and your home are subject to scrutiny. Stringent rules and regulations are required for you and your home. Some rules may seem unnecessary, even extreme, for your situation, but the rules are designed to be all-inclusive, and must be followed for the sake and safety of the child. Fostering normally involves a thorough background check of the prospective foster parents. Friends or family members who may be part-time (respite) helpers are also checked and fingerprinted. Because fostering includes an allowance for food and clothing for the child, foster parents are sometimes accused of taking in children simply for additional income; but really, it is very little money for a lot of work and care.

Until a child reaches age eighteen, the foster child is a ward of the court. In most county systems, this means that a social worker/caseworker visits once a month. The social worker can be employed by a private facility such as a mental health organization that works with the court, but the caseworker is assigned by the court. Under the court system, each child and each biological family has an attorney. If the child is lucky, the court also appoints a child advocate, who has volunteered to supervise and advocate for the child. The caseworker is responsible for the educational rights of the child and is usually an employee of the court system if the biological parent signs off on their educational rights. Everyone has to agree on the best interests of the child. The foster parent and the biological parent are notified of the hearings and invited to attend. The social worker sends a report to the court and gives a recommendation for replacement or retention (a progress report). The home is checked once a year for safety.

ନ୍ତଃ ନ୍ତଃ ନ୍ତଃ

In my experience, the court-appointed attorney for the child read the report of the social worker in the courtroom and agreed with the findings. The court-appointed attorney may have had no other contact with the child or foster parents. As for the educational rights of the child, I have seen those rights violated and the child placed in special day classes without the agreement of the biological parent or caseworker. Most people are not informed about special education requirements that require the least restrictive environment, nor are they aware of their options. When I intervened, the ruling was reversed and the child given help in the regular classroom rather than being placed in a special education class.

Under the auspices of a private agency, the foster parent receives more training, more support and supervision, and more paper work than in the county-based foster system. People involved include a case manager, psychologist, social worker, and family specialist.

In California, training consists of twelve hours covering emotional needs, mandatory rules, regulations and reporting requirements, educational rights, medical responsibilities for the foster parent and the child, response to emergencies, the rights of the biological family, and certified home requirements. Twelve additional hours are required each year.

For foster parents of high-risk children, sixty additional hours of training is required, including intensive family counseling and child abuse mandatory reporting requirements. Eight of the sixty house focus on parenting techniques, love and logic, and six are devoted to possible brain damage from lack of nurturing, fetal alcohol damage and/or drug abuse, though this varies from state to state. Much of the training is usually conducted by professional speakers who use visual aids and stories from real experiences.

ॐ ॐ ॐ

The challenge and joys of foster parenting

Make certain that you are willing to have your life disrupted, because you are opening your heart and home to a person who has been wounded and is frightened. There are many behavioral challenges due to her experiences, and she is emotionally fragile, with a low trust level.

Keep in mind that foster parenting is likely to be only temporary. You must be prepared to love and let go. Many children have had multiple foster parents, and their behavior reflects their knowledge that you, too, will be letting them go. Establish clear boundaries for yourself and the child, because the child has probably had no boundaries until now.

Take care of the caregiver. Always have "respite" people who can spell you. Most members of your extended family will probably back off, because they have no concept of why you are doing this and/or what is happening. All they see is chaos. Reach out to friends, neighbors, and accepting members of your family to get the support you need. You have to be willing to ask for help from anyone and everyone. This means people need to be aware of your foster child's special needs. Anticipate and plan with your neighbors. Once, my foster child blocked my access to the phone because he thought I was calling a social worker. I walked across the street and by pre-arrangement used the neighbor's phone. You need to find one person whose job it is to say to you, "You are doing a fine job." You need to hear this once every day. Remember to eat, rest, and exercise. Keep yourself physically and emotionally healthy so you can continue to meet the challenges of foster parenting.

In interactions with "the system," whatever that system might be—the court, the social worker, the school—it is okay to disagree and dispute advice on occasion. You are with your child twenty-four hours a day. You know intuitively what works and is best for your child. Be an advocate for yourself and your foster child.

ॐ ॐ ॐ

It helps to look for humor and playfulness. Author and speaker Richard DeLani tells the story of a foster child who kept running away. The foster father, the social worker, and even the police would look for him to no avail. The child would watch all this while hiding under a neighbor's porch. When the neighbor discovered this, she told the foster family and they designed a plan. The next time the child ran away, the family got into the minivan and loudly proclaimed, "Let's all get aboard and go for ice cream. It's too bad John isn't here!" Another foster parent tells a story about using humor to change a child's behavior. When she took her foster child shopping, he began to run around, running in and out of clothes racks. When she asked him to come, he only ran deeper into the clothes and hid from her. So she said in a loud and happy voice, "Come here everybody and see these skirts. They are dancing by themselves!"

Building trust is important. Be certain to keep the promises you make. Patience is important. Sometimes, time limits do not allow for building a trusting relationship. Honor the child as an individual and treat him with respect. This builds trust. So does entrusting the child with responsibilities, but only when he can handle those responsibilities and fulfill them successfully.

Trust your common sense and instincts, and determine what is important to you. Identify your child's interests and strengths, and find ways to work with him or her to build on these strengths and interests, whether it be creating a garden or playing with a ball.

"Want your dog to eat your homework?
Add water, and it makes it own gravy."

Keep the rules and values few and simple. Choose the issues you feel are worth fighting for. It is important to remember where the child has been and what she might have experienced. Transitions and new experiences are difficult. Many foster children have experienced post-traumatic stress that will be with them their entire lives, even with years of counseling! "My" child had to have the shower curtain open when he took a shower. He wouldn't sleep in a bed down the hall for the first few weeks. Instead, he slept on the floor near my bed. Gradually, he gained enough sense of security to sleep in his own bed. Some children have come from so many short-term situations, and they come to you with nothing. As they gain toys and clothes, they are reluctant to give them up. Children of the Holocaust slept with bread in their hands. Some foster children have gone to bed hungry and will hoard or steal food, even from the school cafeteria. Overeating and not eating can also occur. In an effort to survive, they frequently lie. In extreme cases, children who have been abused will display abusive behavior themselves with pets or other children. Sometimes they display inappropriate sexual behavior. They have been abandoned, moved, and rejected, and will be constantly testing to see if this will happen again.

$$\mathcal{Z} \quad \mathcal{Z} \quad \mathcal{Z}$$

The joys of foster parenting are probably the same as those of parenting biological children—a hug, a smile, a success. But the intensity is different, due to the nature of the relationship and the child's experiences. Baby steps toward goals are celebrated. Positive responses and behaviors are cherished.

Experiences and relationships taken as commonplace by many parents are slow in coming and are measured as great progress for foster parents. Studies in resiliency have shown that one of the most important factors in overcoming adversity is having one significant adult in a child's life who believed in him. You have the personal satisfaction of knowing that you may be that adult who has contributed to the saving of a life.

Again, I refer to author and speaker Richard De Lani, who told a story to an audience of counselors, social workers, and foster parents about a woman in a wheelchair who, on a hot day, wheeled herself next to a building wall to get some shade. At that very moment above her, a little boy leaned too far out a window. The boy fell onto the woman, which broke his fall. Both were hurt, but both recovered. De Lani ended his presentation with this memorable quote: "Every one of you here is like that woman.

You are catching a child in free fall." That's what foster parents do every day. They are caring for somebody else's child—saving a life by catching a child in free fall.

Summary

Becoming a successful foster parent requires a realistic appraisal of the barriers and builders to success. Before accepting a child into your home, be certain you have the commitment and the behavioral and emotional skills to take on this difficult role. Sometimes, it will be a short-term commitment; sometimes, it could become long-term. Your fostering will be a journey for both you and the child or children, but your commitment and modeling and mentoring may change the destination and certainly make the journey safer and easier for the child.

Chapter 11
Becoming the Parent You Want to Be

*"You don't have to take life the way it comes to you.
By converting your dreams into goals, and your goals into plans,
you can design your life to come to you the way you want it.
You can live your life on purpose."*

Bob Moawad

೫ ೫ ೫

Parenting with purpose has been written around the concept that the kind of adults our children turn out to be is strongly influenced by who we are as adults, the parenting style we choose, the nature of the relationships we establish with our children, the skills and habits we foster, the characteristics we believe are most important to develop, the expectations we set, and values we hold most dear.

Good parenting comes not from trite suggestions and strategies but from becoming parents with personal strength and positive self-esteem. Your effectiveness as a parent can be hampered by your own insecurities, neurotic tendencies, addictions, emotional problems, and low self-esteem. None of us is perfect. This is why we constantly need to invest in our own personal growth.

Feelings that you have about yourself or your self-esteem have a profound impact on all aspects of your life, especially how you raise your children and how they turn out. These feelings affect your energy and enthusiasm, your patience and understanding, and your general mental attitude. This chapter is written to provide you with suggestions for your own personal development, which will enhance your effectiveness as a parent.

ॐ ॐ ॐ

Self-examination

All change begins with self-awareness. Self-awareness sheds light on your existing beliefs and behavior, and should help you understand why you think and act the way you do. It has been suggested that a first step is to recall memories of your childhood, especially those influences and events that had a significant impact on who you are. This includes your upbringing and relationship to your parents, and the significant events and experiences that have occurred up to this point in your life. The following questions might help in that process:

1. What individuals or factors have had the greatest impact on who you are today?
2. What are the beliefs you have about yourself? What are those beliefs based on, and is this information still valid or is it outdated?
3. What statements, comments or criticisms do you remember your parents saying to you as a child?
4. How would you describe your relationship with your mother and your father, and what impact has that had on you?
5. What values do you hold most dear?

ॐ ॐ ॐ

It is important to keep in mind that, while such reflection will add to your self-understanding, it can also determine your behavior, your values, and the goals you set for yourself today. In looking back and gaining insights about your life, you now have a choice in how you want to deal with these insights. You might wish to reject these attitudes and behaviors outright, attribute them to the situation years ago, or put them into proper perspective with other feedback you have received since.

Strengthen your feelings of security

Feeling insecure can significantly limit your functioning. It can keep you from stretching yourself; it can prevent you from risking and trying anything new. It can result in your becoming stuck and afraid to move ahead or step into unknown territory. It is often based on ungrounded fears and anxieties. Can you imagine the courage it took pioneers to venture West or move into areas where wild things abounded? Yet they felt secure enough in themselves to be able to handle those fears and anxieties. Likewise, it is important that you venture forth into uncharted areas in order to grow and become the person you wish to be.

It is important that you face your fears. Don't let them control your life and what you do with it. As Susan Jeffers, the author of *Pack Your Own Parachute*, suggested, "Feel the fear and do it anyway!" Identify all the fears you have, and determine whether they are real or imagined. In most cases, like fear of the dark, our fears are unfounded. It is not things themselves that cause us to feel insecure, but the thoughts we put into our own minds. Try to look at situations realistically for what they are, without making them more frightening than they need to be.

ॐ ॐ ॐ

It may help to make a list of things you are currently worried about. For each item on the list, decide whether you can do something about it, or whether this is a worry that you can let go of because it is out of your control. If you can do something about a worry, then you should not just dismiss it. Take a few minutes to prepare for the event that concerns you, write a note or make a phone call to the person you worry about, or take some step to do whatever you can to relieve that worry. If it is a worry that is out of your control, let someone else deal with it and dismiss it.

To strengthen your sense of security and control, you need to take responsibility for your life, instead of waiting for others or circumstances to determine what happens to you and your family.

You can be the architect of your own happiness by taking positive steps in the direction you want your life to go. It is important to realize that we each have a tremendous source of positive energy within us—when that energy is focused, it can result in better outcomes, positive change, and exciting things happening for us.

Keep in mind that you have a choice in how you want to view life, and how you perceive the circumstances in which you find yourself. Today, many people view themselves as victims. It seems fashionable to feel put upon and downtrodden, to play a passive role and complain about all the unfortunate things that have happened. But you have a choice not to feel that way.

ᏆᏙ ᏆᏙ ᏆᏙ

As an assistant superintendent in a school district, Bob became painfully aware of this choice. He was responsible for the district's instructional division with a staff of 28 specialists, consultants, and administrators. This was at the time of Proposition 13 in California, when the tax base was changed throughout the State. While both he and the superintendent were on vacation, the business manager went to the Board of Education and convinced them the district could no longer afford an instructional division. The business manager encouraged the Board to dismiss or reassign all 28 individuals in his department, leaving Bob with one secretary and the entire work load. Needless to say, he felt discouraged, frustrated, and overwhelmed! The fact that the action had been taken during his absence so he couldn't object to it, was particularly galling! It was then that he realized he had a choice. It was too late to change the decision; but he could remain upset, bitter, and frustrated, or he could make the best of the situation. He decided to take a positive approach and become an expert in all areas of instruction. A year later, a nearby school district asked him to apply for the superintendent vacancy in their district. That is how Bob became a superintendent and where he remained for 12 years. It was an important lesson for him.

You may or may not be in a position to change the circumstances in which you find yourself, but always remember that you do have a choice in how you wish to deal with things. Robert Louis Stevenson is reported to have said, "Life is not a matter of holding good cards, but of playing a poor hand well!"

In many cases, you may be able to improve some aspect of your situation. That might mean taking the initiative to repaint a room, plant flowers, come in with a smile more often, or speak pleasantly to those who seem to ignore you. Taking the initiative is one way to feel better about yourself.

Some activities to consider:

1. Establish routines for yourself to enable you to better organize your time.

2. Plan for some "down time" for yourself to read, meditate, or relax just before you need to deal with your children.

3. Make a list of those things that you are afraid to do, and challenge yourself to engage in at least one of those activities.

4. Define an area where you realize you should take greater responsibility.

5. Keep a record of how much time you spend on different activities during a typical 24-hour period. Compare this with your priorities and what you think this record should look like.

Build a positive self-concept

How you feel about yourself or your self-esteem depends on the discrepancy between the person you wish to be and a realistic assessment of who you are—the greater this discrepancy, the lower your self-esteem. This implies that there are two basic ways to feel better about yourself.

First, be realistic about the expectations you set for yourself. We all have expectations set for us by others, including parents, employers, children, partners, neighbors, and the culture in which we live. It is humanly impossible to live up to all of those expectations. We can't please everyone at the same time. Burnout comes from trying to meet unrealistic expectations. You don't have to live your life pleasing others in order to be a worthwhile person.

☙❧ ☙❧ ☙❧

The best solution is to set your own priorities and decide for yourself which expectations you are going to try to meet, rather than putting yourself down for not meeting all of them. So you can start feeling better about yourself by visualizing the person you wish to be in more realistic terms.

Second, concentrate more on all the positive qualities and strengths you have going for you, or focus on changing and improving those areas where you wish to grow, or combine the two. Either will help to raise your level of personal self-esteem.

Do you tend to discount compliments and your successes because you feel they are nothing out of the ordinary? Do you see yourself as undeserving of happiness? If your answer to these questions is "yes," you need to change your perception of yourself. You may be carrying around negative images or comments from feedback received long ago, which may not be true at all or may no longer apply. You probably have an inner critic or inner voice constantly giving you negative messages. It's that voice that reminds you of your faults and past mistakes, establishes unrealistic expectations for you, points out others who have more expertise or are more attractive than you, and ignores or discounts your accomplishments and positive qualities. If you must examine your faults, don't do so with a magnifying glass, and don't allow your perceptions to color the entire image you have of yourself. Research has determined that as much as 75% of what we think about ourselves is negative, leading us to underrate ourselves and add to our feelings of inferiority.

To make a difference in your life you need to accept yourself as you are now.

Self-acceptance involves acknowledging your strengths and weaknesses and essentially respecting or loving yourself in the face of that information. You may need to change your self-image to fit the Real You. To reduce those old images and silence your negative critic be realistic about the fact that you have multiple strengths as well as aspects that you wish were different. Accept those aspects of yourself which you cannot change, and concentrate on changing those aspects of yourself which are within your power to change. When you base your self-acceptance on reality as it exists today, you can have peace within yourself and begin to bloom into the beautiful parent you were meant to be.

ବ୍ୟ ଡ୍ୟ ବ୍ୟ

Individuals who achieve the greatest success have learned to acknowledge that they are not good in all areas, but have learned how to capitalize on their strengths. So find ways to use your strengths to best advantage. Make your self-talk positive. Visualize yourself as a successful, warm, caring parent.

To think positively about yourself and be an effective parent, strive to function at a conscious level. Work to increase your awareness of the choices, decisions, and actions you make. Be aware of whether those choices, decisions, and actions were made automatically, or whether they were made as really conscious choices. The more frequently you are aware of your options and act on that awareness, the more likely you are to feel better about yourself.

Some activities to consider:

1. Make a list of all individuals who have expectations for you, and write down those expectations. Then go back and place a check mark in front of those that you feel are unrealistic at this particular time of your life. Of the remaining expectations, focus your energy on those that you consider to be top priority.

2. Stand in front of the mirror and look at yourself without judgment. Say to yourself, "This is who I really am right now. I will accept myself as I am now and will work on what I can improve on and accept those imperfections beyond my control."

3. When receiving criticism or anger from your children about a decision you have made related to them, separate the anger or criticism from who you are and the role you have to play as a responsible parent.

4. Begin each day by thinking of three positive things about yourself. End your day by thinking of what went well today and what you are looking forward to for tomorrow.

5. Acknowledge your own feelings. Develop effective ways of dealing with your feelings of anger, hostility, frustration, and depression. Avoid feelings of guilt.

Strengthen your relationships

The need to feel accepted by others and to belong, is basic to human beings. How do you act when in a social group among individuals you do not know? Do you feel comfortable enough to initiate conversations, or do you tend to wait until someone else takes the initiative? To be accepted by others, you must be open and willing to share your ideas, values, priorities, and interests so they can know you better. When individuals hide their emotions and opinions by not expressing them, it makes others feel very uncomfortable. One way to gain friends and acquaintances is to be open about who you are.

Friends are important. Research indicates that those with close friends and a close support group live ten years longer than those who do not have such a group. It is important to keep contact with old friends, including school classmates, former neighbors, and work partners. But developing new friends is also important. This can be difficult, especially if you are new to a well-established community. Sometimes it takes months or even years before you really feel accepted and become an integral part of the group. When you have skills, topics, or interests that you can share with others, you make it easier for them to know you and to feel that they have something in common with you.

☙ ❧ ☙

One way to facilitate this process is to take the initiative to get to really know as many individuals as you can. Ask about their interests, their background, their family, and dreams or aspirations. In doing so, you are likely to find that you have more in common with these people than you ever imagined. A major value in gaining new friends is to expand your personal support group. We all need a strong support group because we lose close friends as we grow older—they may move away, take up new interests, or gain new friends through other groups they join.

Having a personal support group or close friends is especially important to most women. A support group provides an opportunity to share perceptions, news, and concerns. Without close friends, women can easily feel isolated. Those with good mental health typically have a strong group of friends with whom they can share their life experiences. These friends might be old neighbors, college friends, or individuals with whom we work.

View yourself as a member of a team or support group concerned for the welfare of members of the group. When you begin to focus on helping others, you are likely to feel less isolated and less depressed. Take time to engage in being of service to those less fortunate than you are. Being appreciated for the support or help that you have given to someone else is the best way to feel valued. Associate with positive, supportive individuals who recognize your positive qualities and who believe in you.

Make an effort to be a "climate creator." A climate creator is one who changes the environment for others, sometimes by just a smile or a word of thanks. Take time to compliment others and acknowledge their strengths and contributions. Let others know that you appreciate them and what they are trying to do; offer your support to them if they should need it.

Some activities to consider:

1. Make a list of those individuals with whom you have strained relationships. Write a note, make a phone call, or contact each of these people in some way. If the relationship is important to you, go at least halfway to restore it. Then leave it up to the other person to take things from there.

2. Make a list of those people you would like to consider as part of your support group. Be sure to include school friends, neighbors, or others you haven't had contact with recently, to let them know you still consider them important to you.

3. Plan an informal get-together for members of your support group. Engage in a fun activity together.

4. Involve yourself in a community project that is worth your time and energy. For example, you might volunteer your time to your child's teacher or school as a tutor, an aide, or as a clerical assistant.

5. Use a new recipe for a cake or special dish and give it to someone just as a way of saying, "I care." Explain that it is a new recipe and you'd like to get the person's reaction so he or she won't feel obligated to reciprocate.

Quotations to post:

"A friend is one who knows your song and sings it when you forget it."

"Real friends are those who, when you have made a fool of yourself, don't believe that you made a permanent job of it."

"Many people will walk in and out of your life, but only true friends will leave footprints in your heart."

Eleanor Roosevelt

༄ ༄ ༄

Create a compelling vision for your life

Having a clear sense of priorities gives real meaning to your life and gives purpose to your daily activities. These priorities change as your children grow up. You may begin focusing on establishing a home, perhaps try balancing a career and a family, decide to further your education and training, or take on a new responsibility. Even in the midst of changing priorities, however, it is also important to have a long-range vision for yourself and what you'd like to achieve, or the kind of person you'd like to be.

༄ ༄ ༄

To achieve that long-range vision, you must expand your comfort zone, try different activities and open yourself up to new experiences. It's all too easy to get in a habit of doing the same daily activities; but that is likely to lead to depression and frustration. Make an effort to gain new friends, participate in different activities, take on new interests, enroll in a special class, or volunteer to help lead a youth group in which your children are involved. Stepping out of your comfort zone often requires great personal risk. It's natural to feel that you lack the background or expertise to participate equally with others; but participating is the only way you will grow and gain that expertise.

You will grow in direct proportion to the challenges you encounter and engage in, so look for projects that stretch, but don't overwhelm, your abilities. Don't worry about whether you will be successful at the beginning; few people are. Give the new experience a try anyway, and determine what you can learn from that experience. Successful people actually fail more than others, but they benefit from their experiences and move on.

It's important to want to be the best parent you can be, but it's also important to have a vision for yourself to become the kind of person that you ultimately want to be. Unless you have that vision, your only source of satisfaction will to be in your children's accomplishments. That can be hazardous. When they become of age, they will discover that they no longer need you, and leave. This is when it becomes especially important to have a long-range vision for yourself apart from being a parent, though being a parent will always remain a major concern and responsibility. Don't make your children a project that consumes your whole life's energy.

When you have a vision of what you would like to achieve for yourself, begin to set some specific goals that will lead you to that end. These may be short-term or long-term goals. They may take years to accomplish, but will be a first step in giving you perspective on your life.

Some activities to consider:

1. Write down what you hope to accomplish within 5 years, 10 years, and 20 years. Then write down how it would feel to accomplish those goals.

2. Give some thought to what you would have to do, to feel really successful. Then develop a vision for yourself that would give you such feelings of success.

3. What changes do you anticipate happening in your life over the next 5–10 years? What could you do to prepare yourself for those changes?

4. Identify a particular challenge that you would consider taking on, that would expand your knowledge or skills. Set a goal to take on that challenge, even though it may seem scary to think about.

5. Set aside some time during your week to learn a new skill, engage in an interest, read a book, spend time with friends, or do things you don't normally have time for.

Make effective use of your time

How you spend your time has a great deal to do with how you feel about yourself.

Most of us complain that we never have enough time to do all the things we need or desire to do, but there are steps we can take to maximize our use of time.

First, avoid procrastination. Procrastination is a major waste of time that can lead you to spend almost as much time thinking about a task as doing it. Procrastination also is likely to interrupt your concentration while doing other tasks, and it can affect your sleep. Procrastinating also can add to negative feelings you have about yourself, because of the guilt associated with it.

Second, it helps to spend your time on those tasks that you consider to be of highest priority rather than on those tasks that might be handiest or easiest to do. It's important to clarify each day which tasks are most important for you to complete that day. Even if you don't get everything accomplished, at least you will derive satisfaction from having completed those tasks that are most critical.

Third, try to reduce your wasted time. Where do you tend to spend a great deal of your time that doesn't pay off? Is it talking on the telephone with friends, watching TV, browsing through magazines, or surfing the Internet? Each of these activities can be stress-reducing and highly productive when you need time away from other business you need to handle; but they can also take up more time than you really intend to spend on them, unless you are aware of how quickly time passes. These activities can also provide much more enjoyment when you have completed other priority tasks, because then you can fully relax while doing them.

ॐ ॐ ॐ

Studies have indicated that many of the activities that we enjoy provide us with only short-term pleasure. Such activities include watching TV, going to a movie, or playing a card game. Activities that provide long-term enjoyment are those termed "gratification activities," because they leave you feeling that you have accomplished something, contributed, or done something worthwhile. These activities may actually involve hard work, such as working in the garden, practicing a skill, exercising, cooking, sewing, or cleaning out a closet. Studies have found that those who experience the greatest happiness are those who maintain a balance between pleasurable and gratification activities. Individuals who spend most of their time engaging in short-term pleasure activities were found to suffer from significantly more depression.

It is therefore important to give thought to your use of time and how you can schedule your daily activities to give you a greater sense of satisfaction and gratification.

Invest in yourself

The best investment of your time or money is investing in your own personal growth and satisfaction. You are the most important factor in your child's welfare, growth, and mental health. When you fail to invest in your own physical and mental health, your child is likely to suffer. Therefore, it is vital that you take time to exercise properly and meet your other physical and mental health needs. When you are stressed, find ways to restore your inner peace and energy. This might be by taking a walk or by engaging in hobbies or interests such as painting, sculpting, or drawing. It might be by listening to a particular kind of music or by spending time meditating or practicing yoga. It helps if you have a place where you can go by yourself, surrounded by objects that give you pleasure and restore your batteries.

ॐ ॐ ॐ

Critical to your mental health is maintaining a positive outlook on life. Many individuals become cynical and depressed about things that happen to them, but such attitudes can be detrimental to both mental and physical health by adding to stress, depression, and blood pressure. When you make an effort to be optimistic and look at the positive side of life, you are more likely to be successful at things you try to accomplish, and others will enjoy being with you. Surround yourself with individuals who have an optimistic outlook and who are fun to be around.

Decide on ways in which you would like to grow, whether it be acquiring a new skill, a new interest or hobby, or new knowledge. When you invest your time in such activities, you become more capable, you open yourself up to new opportunities, and you increase your enthusiasm for life. Perhaps the greatest payoff to this is having your child experience the joy that comes from investment in personal growth and meaningful activities.

Make a commitment to work on goals that you have set that will enable you to achieve a sense of satisfaction and accomplishment.

These might be short-term or long-term goals or things you have put off that you would give you great feelings of gratification. Taking time for such activities will give your life a sense of purpose and significance.

Finally, take pride in yourself by dressing with pride, walking with pride, and acting like you are proud of who you are. There are no blueprints or models for who you should be. You are commissioned to be a unique, creative individual by virtue of your creation. The greatest contribution you can make to your children is to be fully you and to enjoy who you are.

Some activities to consider:

1. Make a list of the "dead wood" in your life—those things that you keep saying you need to do, like clean out a closet, straighten your desk, organize your schedule. Then do one thing each week to reduce this list.

2. Keep a "Smiley File" composed of thank you notes, inspirational quotes, things that make you smile or laugh.

3. Write down all those things you have achieved that you feel good about and those things others have complimented you on. When you feel down, read over the list to put things into perspective.

4. Keep a journal for writing ideas, a plan of action, and daily successes.

5. Think of something you have done recently that you feel good about. Recall the event vividly in your mind and the pleasure it gave you at the time. Consider the skills and experiences you had to have in order to achieve that.

6. Plan how you wish to celebrate your own accomplishments when you finish something of significance you have been working on.

Achieving a state of wisdom as a parent

Knowledge is information that you have accumulated. No book or amount of knowledge can guarantee that you will be a good parent. Parental wisdom comes over a period of time, pulling together and applying all those things that help you arrive at being an effective parent. The authors of this book hope that the ideas presented here will aid in your growth towards wisdom as a parent. You may never believe that you fully achieve such a state, but ideally you now have some principles on which to base your growth, both as an effective adult and as a competent, loving parent.

Don't expect to be the perfect parent, if indeed such a model could ever exist. We need to view parenting as one of continuous learning. We can't always model a set of exemplary behaviors; and there are no exact formulas for raising children. Even children raised under the same conditions often turn out quite differently.

೦ಆ ಅಂ ೦ಆ

It is important that you have confidence in yourself and that you deal with life in a proactive manner, aware that you have some choices in how you want to deal with the circumstances of life. Don't be fearful of making a decision that might make you seem foolish. The only way to transcend mediocrity is to focus on the values and principles that are most important to you, profit from your poor choices, and then move on, wiser from the experience.

Jonas Salk, the developer of the polio vaccine, is reported to have said that he was brought up in an environment that didn't deal with meaningless absolutes like success, failure, win, lose, or problems. He was only taught to see challenges, situations, and opportunities for making discoveries. Consequently, he was able to benefit from the over two hundred "failed" experiments with polio by analyzing what each experiment taught him. In this way he was able to achieve his vision of a way to wipe out the dreaded disease.

Wisdom comes from establishing the practice of analyzing our experiences to determine what works and what doesn't work, and how we can apply those insights in the future. One thing that must be kept in mind is that once you have found the solution with one child, it may not work at all with a second or third child, so don't get discouraged. You may need to act like you know what you are doing, dealing with your children with confidence and assurance, even when you don't feel that you do. If the decisions you make with respect to your children are based on your deep love for them and in their best interests, your children will most likely accept your decisions and believe that you are a model parent!

Ꙭ Ꙭ Ꙭ

Summary

The five keys of security, identity, belonging, purpose, and competence provide a basis for raising children with values and vision—values on which to base a lifetime of honor, and visions that lead to happiness and success as adults. It has been exciting for us to see so many young people take initiative and responsibility for their lives and turn into highly effective individuals. We believe that by following the model we have outlined and using the activities we have suggested, you will have a greater chance of creating children with soul who are self-actualized and a joy to be with.

Ꙭ Ꙭ Ꙭ

Robert Reasoner

Robert Reasoner has had 50 years of experience in education, serving as teacher, principal and school district superintendent. He is known throughout the world as a pioneer and authority in the field of self-esteem. He founded the California Center for Self-Esteem and has served as president of both the National Association for Self-Esteem and the International Council for Self-Esteem. He has written several books and articles for parents and educators and has served as a consultant and trainer in more than twenty different countries. He is the author of the curriculum *Building Self-Esteem: A Comprehensive Program for Schools*, a program now used widely throughout the world. He was honored by both the Senate and State Assembly of California and was selected as National Educator of the Year in 1992 by the National Association for Self-Esteem and is listed in *Who's Who in American Education*.

Marilyn L. Lane

Marilyn Lane has been a classroom teacher, a teacher of the gifted and talented and a university professor. Administrative roles include being a school principal, a parent education coordinator, and director of gifted education in California and Saudi Arabia. She has held leadership positions as president of the California Association for the Gifted, director of the California Association for Self-Esteem, and vice-president of the National Association for Self-Esteem. Marilyn is a consultant nationally and internationally and has developed curriculum for teachers and parents. She believes her greatest accomplishment and greatest joy is her four grown children and four grandchildren.